UNLOCK THE SECRETS TO YOUR SUCCESS...

Your palmprints, fingerprints, skin patterns, and fingernails are more than individual characteristics...they're the clues to finding your life's work! Through the art of hand analysis, you can discover abilities and talents you never knew you had—and career choices you never dreamed of. With this fascinating guide, you can learn about your...

- Skills, ambitions, and interests
- Personality and temperament
- Vocational aptitudes
- Career directions
- Goals and educational opportunities
- Career motivation

   And much more!

Berkley Books by Beverly Jaegers

BEYOND PALMISTRY

BEYOND PALMISTRY II: YOUR
CAREER IS IN YOUR HANDS

BEYOND PALMISTRY II:

YOUR CAREER IS IN YOUR HANDS

BEVERLY JAEGERS

B

BERKLEY BOOKS, NEW YORK

BEYOND PALMISTRY II: YOUR CAREER
IS IN YOUR HANDS

A Berkley Book / published by arrangement with
the author

PRINTING HISTORY
Berkley edition / May 1996

ISBN: 0-425-15296-0

BERKLEY®
Berkley Books are published by The Berkley Publishing Group,
200 Madison Avenue, New York, New York 10016.
BERKLEY and the "B" design
are trademarks belonging to Berkley Publishing Corporation.

PRINTED IN THE UNITED STATES OF AMERICA

10   9   8   7   6   5   4   3   2   1

This book is dedicated to
my inspiration and chief critic,
my husband Ray;
my friend and agent, Kay McCauley;
to Joan Bramsch, without whom
nothing would have progressed;
to my editor, Judy;
to Neil; Mike; Phyllis; Syd; Dena; Vivian;
and all of those who have believed in me.

CONTENTS

INTRODUCTION

How often have you heard another person say, "I hate my job. I wish I could do something I like!"? Perhaps the man or woman at the next desk shows boredom and dissatisfaction with what he or she is doing; or perhaps *you* find it harder and harder to rise each morning to return to a job you despise.

Surveys taken by leading magazines and newspapers have confirmed that a great number of today's workers would much rather be doing anything other than what they are doing.

Vocational analysis and aptitude tests have apparently flunked out in discovering who has "the right stuff" for any job. Career counseling is often neglected until college, and even at that level, students often find they have completed two or more years of work toward a liberal arts degree with no specialization in mind at all. Others, having plunged into a field that held some interest for them at one time, suddenly find themselves near the end of their educational years with no options remaining.

Is there a remedy? Perhaps more broadly applied and timely skills analysis testing might be instituted in either grade or high school; or complete psychological, personality, and vocational testing might be added to the usual SAT scores. Even these methods, however, may lack the fine-tuning needed to fit the individual into the exact niche where he or she will fit.

As a hand analyst for more than thirty years, I have found that as a method of analyzing career and job skills, analysis of your own hand from an inked print can supply you with a sure and complete index of your specific skills, talents, and abilities. I have seen the motor skills and scientific aptitude of an astronaut disregarded and suppressed because a dominating father, president of a large corporation, insisted his son follow him into the executive suite of a staid corporation. I have discovered the potential of great writers, artists, and teachers, seen the earmarks of a fine, if not great, actress compressed into the confines of a librarian's book-filled world—just because her librarian mother wanted her child to follow her own pathway.

I have often seen the hand of a computer genius, a research scientist, or a natural pilot whose potential was overlooked and discarded because of a parent's overpowering will, or just through lack of knowledge that special talents existed.

Some twenty years ago, a young man, Charley, came to me with a project in mind that was consuming his college summers. He and a few friends planned to buy and refurbish an abandoned railroad caboose somewhere in the west, creating a unique restaurant for the small community in which they located it. He was oblivious to anything other than that idea. Yet when I looked at his big and capable hands I saw not a restaurateur, but a teacher; not an unfulfilled life in that trackless western desert, but a vigorous and exciting life in a very specialized field of agricultural exploration. There were also indications of life in another country, and of a facility in speaking Spanish.

But when I told Charley what his hand indicated about his potential, he laughed and rejected all of it, happily going back to his caboose and his project.

Then, almost five years later, the telephone rang on my desk and a vibrant male voice began to tell me that he, the budding caboose owner, had changed his educational path and was at present working in Honduras, instructing the native people how to repair and use their U.S.-donated tractors, and giving them aid in crop planning as well. Of course, he also had to learn to speak fluently the dominant language in Honduras: Spanish.

He just wanted me to know.

Over the years, Charley has sent me a good many others who found themselves in the wrong job and needed to know what their hands could reveal.

Perhaps not everyone will find such a wide divergence between what he or she *is* doing and what he or she *should* be doing, but it is undoubtedly true that most of us have little or no idea of the wide range of skills and talents we already possess!

Analyzing your hand may not be the magic Aladdin's lamp to instantly change your job as a used-car salesman into a career as a Hollywood movie director, but it is certain that when you find out just what fields you should have pursued, and spend some time in reeducation, many avenues that would have remained closed to you will open automatically, giving you another chance at the brass ring of life!

Do you find yourself groaning out loud as you pull into that last parking place each morning? Do you stare at yourself in the fogged-up bathroom mirror after your shower, mentally seeing yourself as a belly dancer in Bali, or a sailor following trade winds off the Kona Coast?

Then dive right into the world of your hand, and begin to find the person you know the least about—yourself!

WHAT YOU WILL NEED TO BEGIN

Hand analysis begins with an inked handprint of one or both of your hands. You will need:

A tube of Speedball water-soluble block printing ink, black
A 2″ or 3″ rubber roller
(Both of these are available at any art store or hobby shop)

A tile or piece of smooth plastic to roll ink on
A folded tea towel or sheet of spongy plastic
20 lb. or heavier white paper

Do not wash the hands before printing them. Ordinary skin oils help the hand to print clearly. Lotion may be used after the prints are made.

1. Both hands may be printed at the same time if you have someone to help you; if you are alone, print the dominant hand (the one used most) and then print the other hand.
2. Squeeze a half-inch of ink out on the tile or a plate.
3. Roll the ink smoothly in a medium-size circle.
4. Hold the roller in the left hand and gently roll the ink onto the surface of the right palm.
5. When the entire palm and fingers are covered, place a sheet of paper on top of the folded towel and put the hand down onto the paper briefly, pressing lightly.
6. Lift the hand to see if the print is clear.
7. If the ink looks heavy and you cannot see the fingerprints and skin patterns clearly, put a second piece of paper down and make a second print before the ink dries too much.
8. If the ink is too dry, roll more ink onto the hand, then print it again.

When you have a clear print, sign and date the paper for future reference.

Looking at the prints in this book will give you a clear idea of what a handprint should look like.

Most people have hands of similar size and shape, although the dominant hand, usually the right, may be a bit larger. This size differential also extends to the feet, which is the reason a shoe sales person will try the right shoe on first, as he or she knows that if it fits, the left foot will fit, too.

1

THOSE FASCINATING FINGERPRINTS

Hand analysis is the finest vehicle of self-discovery known to mankind. More personal than the stars, more specific than handwriting, the hand provides in its skin patterns, shapes, and sizes a perfect reflection of you, with all your good points as well as those not so welcome.

Although the lines on your hand can and do change as you change, the shape of hand and fingers is slower to reflect differences in your life. Skin patterns, of course, are formed at the end of the first three months of prenatal life, and can never change. Theoretically, these skin patterns are formed by and contain an index of all your inherited traits, drawn from all of your ancestors. In fact, they are thought to be the visible signature of the DNA.

All of us draw upon the accumulated skills and talents of those who came before us, and we often put several of these aptitudes together to create something entirely new. In the earlier years of this century, computers were only dreams and technology was still in its infancy, so how could you be a born

Loop

Loop prints indicate a fast-moving intellect with quick responses. They belong to people-oriented individuals.

Tented Arch

Tented arch prints signify the sort of mind that asks questions. Less outwardly oriented, this person is introspective but not shy. He is always asking for information to feed his insatiable curiosity about everything.

computer programmer if you draw only upon your ancestors? Can a rocket engineer be the result of a long line of farmers or cattlemen? Yes, of course, this is possible, as it may well be that one or more of these ancestors took a step beyond the ordinary, perhaps had a hobby of mixing his or her own chemicals to use upon the soil, or devised some improved method of breeding the perfect Hereford. Perhaps a female ancestor lent her skills at distilling medicines and cordials from garden herbs and plants or concocting dyes to make her quilts and clothing different and distinctive, for you to draw upon today. The result could be a knack for chemistry in your own nature, or just an enhanced interest in the processes of science.

These skin patterns are indelible, infallible indicators of all of your personal ambitions, skills, and even your interests.

Most fascinating of all are the completely individual prints

Plain Whorl

Plain whorls are found on individuals who are intense and able to concentrate. They may indicate some area of specialization. They also show insight. One would never lie to another person who had a whorl on his or her index fingertip.

Double Loop

Double loops may mark an area of personality that shows an unusual aspect. Slower to act than others, people with such a mark must think and inspect before they react.

on the tips of your fingers, as these delineate your special outlook on life.

Five months before a human child is born, the loops and swirls of the fingerprints and palmar lines appear on the developing fetal hands. At that time the brain is beginning to take on a functional capacity and individuality. More complex than similar patterns on the bottoms of the feet, these skin patterns are referred to as dermatoglyphics (skin carvings) and appear to be genetic markers outlining the biological heritage of the child yet to be born.

The combinations of finger patterns are unique, and no duplicate patterns have ever been recorded on any two human hands.

Footprints taken in hospital birthing suites mark the identity of the child, but the largest collection of identifying hand and fingerprints resides in the computer banks belonging to the

Fingerprint Patterns

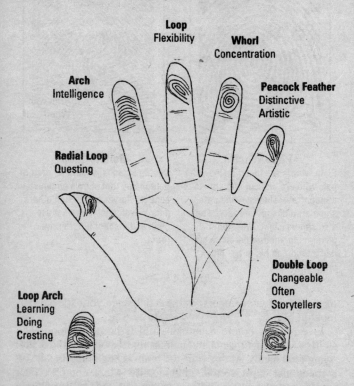

Loop
Flexibility

Whorl
Concentration

Arch
Intelligence

Peacock Feather
Distinctive
Artistic

Radial Loop
Questing

Double Loop
Changeable
Often
Storytellers

Loop Arch
Learning
Doing
Cresting

FBI, Interpol, Scotland Yard, and the newer NCIC (National Crime Information Computer).

Although finger and handprints and their undoubted ability to identify any human, living or dead, have been collected since the mid-1860s, no effort had ever been made before then to ascertain whether they had any meaning!

Hand analysts categorize fingerprints into seven or eight groups that indicate skills and talents.

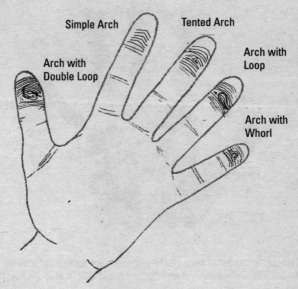

Simple Arch

Tented Arch

Arch with Double Loop

Arch with Loop

Arch with Whorl

Arched Prints

ARCHED FINGERPRINTS

Prints that show an arched formation of skin patterning running horizontally from side to side on the fingertip are categorized according to several types of arches.

These arches are easy to recognize, and are almost always found on the hands of those who are possessors of a developed curiosity. In older times, a person who was prone to ask a great many questions and to search far afield for information was said to have a "curiosity bump." This is the hallmark of arched fingerprints.

If your index fingertip contains an arch, you are always involved in learning something. This is the most common placement of the arched print. It is rare to find arches on the other three fingers or on the thumb.

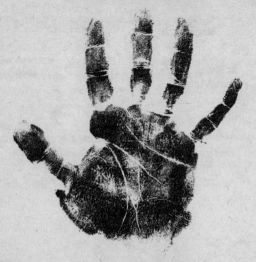

This young hand is of the action type, note wide-spread fingers and thumb. The arched index is an inherited family trait. A loop-arch on the thumb is her own.

This arched index is usually found on the hands of those who learn, study, and do research. Career choices might include writing; designing; scientific research; computer design creating; research assistant; archaeology, paleontology, or one of the other *Ologies*; physician; and medical researcher.

Arched prints indicate the information collector.

TENTED ARCH

An arch that has a wedge-shaped kernel in the middle of the arch pattern is known as a tented arch. The pattern humps up in the center over the tiny kernel. Some of these arches have low kernels of small size, while others look like small posts holding the middle of the pattern upward.

Tented arches belong to the detective, the corporate troubleshooter, law enforcement or criminal justice personnel, even to judges and others interested in the law, especially if that tip section of the index finger is the largest section on the finger.

Other career choices would include journalist; reporter; medical researcher or pharmacologist; highway patrol; security; FBI, CIA, ATF, Justice Dept. etc.; and novelist, including writers of historical fiction or biographers.

LOOP ARCH

This fingerprint looks as if a small, flattened loop rather than a kernel had been inserted between the layers of the arch.

This print formation is commonly found on any of the five fingertips. It indicates a busy and active mind, with a strong

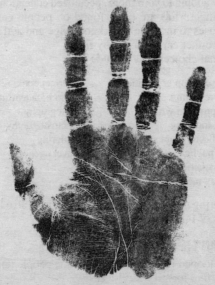

This hand has an unusual arch-loop print on the index finger. The remaining prints are ordinary loops.The owner is a former salesman whose hobby was the study of homeopathic medicines. He now owns a company specializing in distributing these items to the public.

interest in new knowledge and, at times, in exploring the unknown.

If the loop is very small, it belongs to the person who has a strong interest in a great many fields, but may not specialize in any one of them. It may be hard for you to settle down in one career if this print is on your hand, but fortunately other indications on the hand may provide more information.

Career choices indicated might be science, the arts, an area of specialized medicine, social work, forensic medicine, and paralegal work.

If the loop is larger, but still less than one-half the height of the entire fingertip, the mind is less concentrated and leads to a wider variety of interests and creativity. You may find that you evolve naturally from one career to a higher specialty, and are continually adding to your more specialized education as you go.

These fingerprints are often found on people entering college campuses to increase their knowledge and add to specializations in either career or hobby fields.

Vocational choices may include

Publishing, desktop or traditional
  Writing, reporting
Television program writing,
  editing, producing
Antique collecting and sales
Newsletter publication
Medical specialties, such as
  emergency medicine

Gourmet cooking
Radio broadcasting
Photography
Cinematography
Exploring
Travel agency

Engineering or architectural specialties may also be in focus for owners of this fingerprint.

ARCH WITH DOUBLE LOOP

Double-looped prints may puzzle some people until they are able to learn to identify them clearly.

Double loops act as a sort of catch basin for thoughts. They belong to people who are so involved with thinking that they may see all possible sides of any given problem. Because of this, they may get a lot less done than they would wish.

As school children these people might have been considered "slow" or troublemakers, even dreamers, as they are usually off on another mental level, or so it seems, and may not be specifically paying attention to what is going on.

Double loops may sometimes represent one or another area of what would be considered genius in the individual, but can be a big problem during childhood as they chafe under the restrictions of regular rules and ordinary tasks.

The arch formation adds a measure of practicality to the often feckless double loop, so that the owner may be more open to outside stimulus.

Career choices might include

Electronics	Special effects production
Computer systems	Writing fantasy or science
Owning a business	fiction
Invention of new devices	Fantasy art
Modelmaking for production of	Fashion or jewelry design
a sci-fi movie	Avant-garde artist
Unusual types of photography	

This is a most unusual print and must be considered not only for what it is, but also for which fingertip on which it is found. (See chapter 6 on finger sections.)

ARCH WITH WHORL (BULL'S-EYE)

Most unusual of all prints, this is an uncommon formation on any finger. It may represent a genetic tendency toward violence, and although we do not yet know everything about this formation, it is clear that it belongs to persons who may be unsatisfied all of their lives if they are not following the proper career path.

If you have this print on any finger and always wanted to be a veterinarian, for instance, but were unable to afford the extra years of college, you may seem to be able to forget about your most desired career and go into something else entirely, but you will always have the miserable, nagging feeling that you have somehow missed the train and are running to catch up.

If this print appears on your hand, you should seriously consider going back and finding out what field in which you should have been putting your effort. Then begin a reeducation program that will fit you for a career change in the future. Only in this way will you ever find contentment.

Career choices for this fingerprint are almost unlimited by the imagination. They might include fine arts, poetry, furniture restoration, interior design, writing for television, and playwriting.

Whorls are always a sign of concentration on one specific aspect of something. It is difficult for anyone with a whorl print, even an arched print with a whorl inside, to follow anyone else's rules. Salvador Dalí had several, as did famed Thor Heyerdahl, who sailed the raft *Kon Tiki* to discover ancient intercontinental sea routes that showed how prehistoric man may have reached distant shores.

KEY WORDS: INTELLIGENCE, CREATIVITY

LOOP FINGERPRINTS

According to most studies, the loop is the most common of all formations on fingertips. Statistically, Scotland Yard's studies show them to be the largest of all print categories. Their figures, however, are based on a population that consists of a large proportion of Anglo-Saxon people, but few other races.

Prints in the United States show much less uniformity. In fact, as in a true melting pot, the prints reflect the rich racial and cultural-heritage blend we possess in America.

Loops, then, are only slightly more common than other print formations.

Ordinary loops, which have a pattern that enters the fingertip from the little-finger side of the hand, loops around in a tight swirl and then leaves on the side from which it came, are commonly found on one or more fingers of a hand. Although some fingers may have no loops at all.

There are several fingerprints that might be classified as

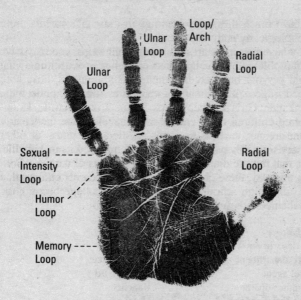

Loop/
Arch

Ulnar
Loop

Radial
Loop

Ulnar
Loop

Sexual
Intensity
Loop

Radial
Loop

Humor
Loop

Memory
Loop

An Inked Handprint—Some Unusual Loops

loops that should not be considered true loops at all. These would include the arch with loop patterns discussed above.

Loops indicate a fast-moving sort of mind, quick to react and with a normal attention span. These people do possess curiosity, but it will not have the depth that is peculiar to those persons with arched fingerprints. Loops indicate persons who may prefer to get their news from TV rather than a newspaper, who may enjoy talk shows and perhaps tabloid TV as well. This cannot be considered a fault, but represents a less intense interest in life outside the personal boundaries of self and friend-family interrelationships.

A loop may be classified as a loop when it seems to span almost the entire top to bottom of the fingertip section. Loops may be found on other finger sections and on the palm itself, but have much different meanings in those placements, both psychologically and vocationally.

If your fingerprints are all or mostly all loops, you may have had a problem until the last years of high school deciding what would be your best career, although as youngsters those with looped fingers often dream of careers as firemen, policemen, and G-men. Girls see themselves as nurses or ballerinas. Loop-fingered children often choose toys that illustrate these early career dreams, such as toy guns, soldiers and tanks, or other military toys if boys, or if girls, small nurses' kits or babylike dolls that require diapering, feeding, and lots of care.

In this way, these children are exhibiting career choices that will, after high school or a few years of college become the actual careers they will follow. These include

MALE:

Fire department
Police department
Travel agent
Computer operator
Construction trades
Electrician
Government service
Social work
Insurance companies
Accountant, CPA
Corporate executive

Journalist
Armed forces
Coast guard
Rancher
Hotel employee
Dentist
Optical technician
Photography lab
Maintenance
Trucking or delivery (UPS)
Postal worker

FEMALE:

Nursery school
Cosmetician
Store clerk
Social work
Computer operation
Policewoman
Paramedic (and EMT)
Media employee
Nurse
Medical assistant

Police dispatcher
Airline hostess
Receptionist
Telephone sales
Dental technician
Personnel
Employment agency
Boutique salesperson
Printing
Schoolteacher

Of course there are a great many other possible careers, many of which can be determined by other aspects of the hand.

Loops indicate normal intelligence with some aspects of creativity. If you have loops on most of your fingertips, you have probably worked at several types of job during your lifetime. Most of these jobs will have been in some field related to human service.

You may have had a problem deciding until late in high school and then followed an early dream career.

Constant, trustworthy, you are among the most reliable and stable of workers, as long as you have made a correct choice of job.

Persons with looped prints may be considered the backbone of the country, as they form the largest segment of the work force at any time. They are also the hardest hurt by cutbacks, and if this is something that has happened to you or you feel it is about to happen, it would be smart to move into some area of specialization as soon as possible, even if you must retrain or reenter college to acquire these abilities.

PEACOCK-FEATHER LOOP

A looped print that seems to be enclosed by a single line is known as a peacock-feather loop. It looks a lot like the famed feather from this colorful bird, although the pattern runs sideways across the fingertip. When you have inked your hand according to the instructions in the introduction to this book, you may turn the sheet with your print sideways to see how this print resembles the shape and "eye" of that feather. The eye will occur at the end of the loop where the sharply curving lines enclose the pattern. The pattern then follows a line straight back to the little finger side of the hand. (See illustration.)

The remainder of the fingerprint may resemble a broad, plain-looped formation, or may look like arched formations above the "feather" itself.

This fingerprint is somewhat rare, but is found on the hands of individuals who have a particular flair of some kind, a special talent.

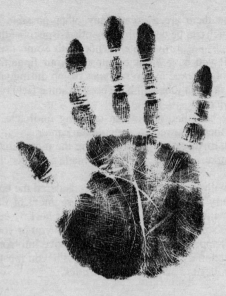

This handprint has an arch with whorl on the middle finger. The little finger is adorned with a loop-arch fingerprint, the perfect peacock-feather formation. Index and ring fingers have a higher whorl. This individual, age forty-two, has changed careers several times. All careers were in service professions.

Career choices may vary widely, or remain in one general area, such as

Social worker/specialized areas

Service professions (police, fireman, nurse)

City planner/Government

Contractor/Builder/Architect

Writer/Journalist/Successful Author

Home security expert/Company owner and chief designer

Antiques dealer/Restorer

Auctioneer/Specialist in antiques history and techniques

Artist/Illustrator/Fine Arts

Corporate troubleshooter/ Highly Paid Consultant

Multitalented handyman/Contractor

As is indicated, if you have this fingerprint on one or more of your fingers, you may take training in an entry-level job in some field that appeals to you; then when you have conquered this you will begin to learn more and to specialize within that field.

Peacock-feather fingerprints belong to those who cannot stand a do-nothing, dead-end job. They will always climb toward the top.

Check Chapter 6 on finger sections for a more specific look at the basic field preferences.

KEY WORDS: DISTINCTIVE, ARTISTIC, MULTITAL-ENTED

RADIAL LOOP

Another unusual print is the loop that seems to enter and then leave the finger from the thumb side of the hand, rather than the little-finger side. This is known as a radial loop, from the radial bone in the forearm, and is uncommon on any finger except the index.

Radial loops indicate a person who is a learner, a seeker after the knowledge of others, and very particular about his or her sources. While ordinary ulnar loops, entering and leaving from the little-finger side, belong to those who like to follow natural paths through life, radial loop people will take the ideas and pathways of others and create a new and special highway of their own.

Like the peacock-feather, radial loops belong to those who will choose specialization in any field.

If you have a radial loop on your index fingertip, you will have spent many happy hours listening to those who have excelled in their fields, and then eventually you will choose to follow in the footsteps of one of these masters and build your own ideas upon that foundation.

You will always find it difficult to work in any job that constricts your time or your physical activity to a routine of any kind. If you have a desk job, you will need to balance this with extra breaks or periods of walking outdoors. You are not likely to be happy tied to a time clock, or to enjoy any job that limits your freedom of action or thought.

Career choices depend largely on the basic aptitudes of the entire hand. In many cases, the profession you end up in will be one you have created yourself.

Media	Trial lawyer
Consultant/Troubleshooter	Real estate developer
Computer designer or systems planner	Import-export specialist
Artist in some unusual medium	Actor (This could be a hobby rather than a profession)
Sculptor/Mural painter	Landscaping
Pilot, test pilot, or astronaut	Botany/Forestry/Park Ranger
Inventor/Designer	Some areas of science or religion
Financial planner	

If found very small on the index finger, this loop signifies that you are one who prefers to do your own thinking. You would do well to find some career in which you can be your own boss, set your own hours, and work at your own pace, as you do not like to take orders.

If the loop is very large, you are more likely to gain from the experience of others and are not afraid to ask questions in order to learn.

KEY WORDS: QUESTING, SEEKING

LOOP PRINTS

This combination of loop and arch may puzzle you until you decide into which category it fits. To be a true looped arch, the loop portion must be at least half the height of the fingertip or larger. This loop is usually quite large and may curve upward almost to the tip of the finger. The arching lines that enclose it at top and bottom must be the smaller portion of the finger-print.

Most loops enter gently from the little finger and in a wide, curving swing, then gradually loop back to where they entered. There will be no kernel, as kernels belong to the peacock-

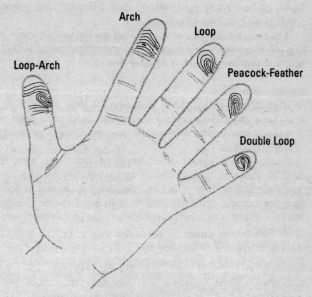

Larger Loop-Arches

feather formation. There may be a small closed oval in the center position, but this will be long and thin.

If you have this print on one or all of your fingers, you have a busy and active mind, with a strong interest in new knowledge during your childhood, and again in retirement years.

You are intrigued by the unknown or mysterious, but also a little afraid of it. Normally a traditionalist, you are likely to belong to a church and one or more social groups, clubs, or associations.

You may have considered a career as a secondary goal, if female, and believed that your most important goal was to be a successful wife and mother. If male, you accepted marriage and family with a responsible attitude.

You may have married a childhood or high-school sweetheart, and not completed your education beyond high school or the first year or two of college.

You may be in a career you did not prefer, or in a lower paying job you hate, while hoping that something better will come along if you are patient. You have one or more hobbies.

If this is the case, a careful analysis of your hand should be extremely helpful.

It is important for those with several loop fingerprints on both hands to make a careful analysis of their entire hand, with a realistic assessment of even the smallest vocational direction it can give them.

I have seen this print on the hands of many who were stuck in jobs, just waiting for retirement so that they could then follow their hearts. It is possible, however, for anyone to prepare him- or herself carefully and then make a career change in midlife. What is required is the choice, the preparation, and the will to do so.

Career choices might include

Crafts	Business Owner
Cabinetry or model-making	Antiques mall operator
Real estate	Part-time performer
Interior coordinator	Bridal gowns and veils
An outdoor or active science such as archaeology	Tanning parlor or spa operator
	Physical therapist
Rehabbing older homes for resale	Chiropractor/Health specialist
Teacher/Instructor	Author
Specialist/Consultant	

What is important is to discover what you already possess as a result of your career to date, and what latent skills and abilities you can build upon for the future.

I have seen this print on the hands of astronauts and on oceanographers; dog groomers and commodity speculators; antiques appraisers and professional masseuses. All unusual careers, to be sure, yet they were not the original jobs these people took after education was complete. They were the outgrowth of the deepest desires of people frustrated with stale or unsatisfying lives.

What matters most is for you to enjoy getting up to face each day, and to look forward to a career you really like.

KEY WORDS: FLEXIBLE, INVOLVEMENT, INTERESTED

FLARED LOOPS

There is a separate, very small category of loops that enter the hand and then flare upward, reaching toward the tip of the finger.

This loop print belongs to those who see life clearly and who usually settle into a position in which they can advise others in one way or another. It may be in personnel work or corporate headhunting, in teaching or metaphysical classes.

If this is your print, you are best placed in helping your fellows to see themselves more clearly.

WHORLS (BULL'S-EYES)

Whorls look exactly like a bull's-eye on the fingertip! They represent a concentration in the area of life or the personality outlined by that fingertip.

Whorls are among the most uncommon of fingertip markings, and are an inevitable indication of the unusual mind— even an offbeat type of personality that marches to its own music—always the individualist.

Bull's-eyes are also a sign of intensity, willpower, and strength. Although it would be unusual indeed to find a hand whose fingertips were all whorl prints, I have seen quite a few in my thirty-some years of looking. And they were always on the hands of people who were unique in one or many ways.

A hand with all whorls would indicate a person who not only can and usually does make his or her own rules for life and living, but also just cannot manage to conform with the rigid, prosaic rules of society.

Normally found on the index and ring finger, where it is considered a special mark of almost psychic insight, the whorl

Key to Whorl or Bull's-eye Fingerprints

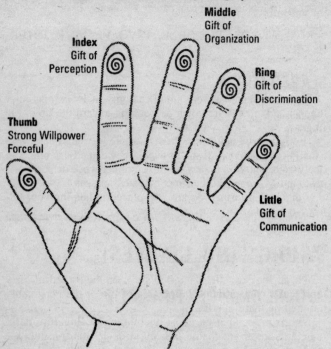

Middle
Gift of
Organization

Index
Gift of
Perception

Ring
Gift of
Discrimination

Thumb
Strong Willpower
Forceful

Little
Gift of
Communication

may be seen on any of the fingertips. Wherever it appears, it indicates an outlook and an attitude essentially all your own in that particular area of life.

I have seen this print on, among others, an ex-cop now driving an armored truck, the owner of a New Age supply shop, a career diplomat at the United Nations, a radio talk show personality, and an author of historical novels. Quite an assortment indeed, and the only thing these people had in common was that their lives, their routines, their attitudes, and their opinions were as different from most other people as if they were, like Mr. Spock, former residents of the planet Vulcan!

Vocational choices:

Any business run and/or owned by the proprietor	Sportsman or woman
	Dollmaker
Reporter	Private investigator
Writer	Bodyguard
Magician	Musician
Actor in films, plays, or TV	Costume designer
Photographer's model	Entrepreneur
Artist in an unusual medium	Inventor
Glassblowing or metalworking	Systems engineer
Designer or decorator	Fashion Artist

Whatever the career, the bull's-eye print adds its own unusual and very personal touch to the life you live.

KEY WORD: INDIVIDUALISTIC

WHORL ON INDEX FINGERTIP

This whorled print is called the gift of perception, because it is the mark of one who sees things clearly. If this print appears on your hand, you cannot be lied to and you see people as they are, not as they would like to appear to be. You can make extremely good character assessments.

If you have only this single bull's-eye on your hand, you would be outstanding in any career that requires "people sense." Personnel, psychological clinical work, and job training and placement work might be your place to shine, or any field where knowing or sensing the truth about people is required.

You may have found this ability to see beyond false fronts, a big problem when you were young, as most of us would prefer to wear rose-colored glasses when it comes to those about us; but as an adult looking for the right career, this could be the single most positive thing you have to offer an employer.

Careers:

Personnel	Office manager
Corporate headhunter	Sales manager
Military recruiter	Psychologist
Lawyer	Psychiatrist
Religious	Internal medicine
Artist/Portraitist	Psychiatric nurse
Architectural consultant	Paramedic/EMI

KEY WORD: PERCEPTION

MIDDLE FINGERTIP

A whorl here is unusual, yet hand analysts do find them from time to time. They are known as the gift of organization, for those who have them are often specialists in arranging and correlating. If you have this fingerprint, you can easily find organization in what others would term chaos. You might see hidden relationships between things that seem entirely different.

You love to do things your own way, and although your desk may appear cluttered, you can find, with one fingertip, anything that is asked for.

This ability to organize can be a tremendous asset in job placement. You merely look for a job that involves putting things or people into the right places!

Your career might be

Computer design	Forensic medicine
Financial analyst	Archaeology
Stockbroker or consultant	Anthropology
Certified public accountant	Paleontologist
Biologist	Museum curator
Anthropologist	Aerospace engineer

This fingerprint almost always belongs to one who has followed one career during the first portion of his or her life, but may have completely changed focus in later life, and begun a whole new career.

KEY WORD: SPECIALIZATION

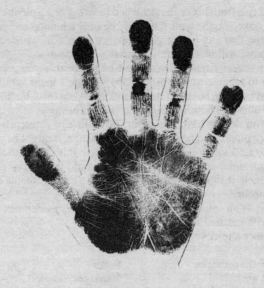

This technical, emotional hand, exhibits four bull's-eye (whorl) prints, on thumb, index, ring, and little fingers. It is the hand of a fifty-three-year-old New Orleans police detective who was a genius at character assessment. His hobby was joining with Midnight Blues musicians along the Crescent City's Bourbon Street.

RING FINGER

A whorl here is not unusual, but what is unusual is the personality and skills it represents. It is called the gift of discrimination, for if you have it, you possess a fine sense of not only what is good for you, but what is good for others as well. In any form of social or governmental work, this would be an invaluable asset.

This whorl also gives you the ability to look at a plan or an object and immediately detect any flaws or loose ends it may have.

People with this whorl are often described as the type who

would rise from his or her deathbed to straighten a picture hanging crooked on the wall. This may be only a humorous idea, but it is true that any out-of-place item or even a misspelled word on a page will immediately jump to your attention.

In a career situation, you must be aware that you are never going to be able to conform to anyone else's ideas about what should be done, but must devise a plan of your own. For this reason it might be best to design and create a business of your own.

If you do not have this whorl or bull's-eye fingerprint, and you are planning a new career or job change, it might be a good idea to find someone else who does have this print and ask his or her opinion about your idea. You would then receive some invaluable insights and might be able to avoid problems before they occur.

This is an interesting fingerprint that always denotes a person with unusual insight.

Career choices:

Vocational counselor	Editor
Social work	Marriage counselor
Politician	Minister or priest
Job counselor	Biographer
Psychologist	Novelist
Stage director	Investor
Costume designer	Lawyer or paralegal
Guidance counselor in a school	Insurance sales or planning

KEY WORD: DISCRIMINATION

LITTLE FINGER

This placement of the whorl print usually indicates someone who utilizes communication as his or her window to the world. When I was on a national television program, the host, Regis Philbin, chose a complete skeptic from the audience for me to print and analyze. I found a whorl on his little finger as well as a very long and well-developed index fingertip. I looked at the print and began telling the man he had an attraction to the law or to justice, and that he had probably sung professionally some time in his life. The man positively jumped in amazement, and the host looked a bit miffed at his skeptic's reaction. The facts were that this man was a police officer, studying for his master's degree in criminal justice, and for nine years had sung as a soloist in a boys' choir.

This whorl will always involve you in some form of reaching outward and communicating with the world. Singing may not be your best choice, but perhaps just talking or writing would be a better choice.

Career options:

Radio or television	Politics
Musician	Teaching or instructing
Singer	Foreign language specialist
Poet	Communications expert
Writer of books or plays	Artist
Advertising Agency	

If you have this print and have chosen another career but would like to communicate more widely, you could consider amateur theatricals, or even just reading books onto tapes for the blind.

Note: It is vitally important that you look for a partner with whom you can communicate before entering into a business or a marriage. Lack of communication will stifle you and eventually cause unhappiness and despair.

KEY WORD: COMMUNICATION

THUMB

Not often seen on the thumb, the whorl adds power to any hand on which it is found in this area. Thumbs are the area of individuality and willpower, so a whorl here could make a big difference in your effectiveness.

This whorl is known as the gift of willpower and forcefulness, as it lends concentration to the *force* you exert on your environment and those around you. No person with a whorled thumb could ever be considered a nerd. (Unless the person wanted to be seen in that way for some reason of his or her own.)

Not especially a mark of the egoist, this print may be seen on the hands of those who choose to lead from behind the throne rather than on it.

If you have this bull's-eye pattern on your thumb tip. It's a good bet that whatever your profession, you will be reaching for the top!

If you have this fingerprint, you may be an individual with the highest of goals for yourself, but you will require that your closest friends and associates be people of the same high ambition. You will stand up for them, but most of all, you feel that you must be true to yourself.

Careers:

Military	Police or military police
Pilot	Surgeon
Business owner	Zoologist
Charity executive	Musician
Teacher or instructor	Composer
Architect	Orchestra or band leader
Astronaut or space technician	Writer

It is also true that whatever you do choose as a career, you will strive to be as good as you can be at whatever it is you are doing.

KEY WORD: FORCEFULNESS

DOUBLE LOOP PRINTS

This very unusual print might be both an asset as well as a liability.

It belongs to those who think deeply, or those who choose not to think at all and to react to the moment. Since it is a loop that doubles back upon itself, it can represent a mind that does the same thing. On some hands, it might indicate an individual who prefers thought to action. In others, it may indicate that things must be thought out to a conclusion and all advice sought before something is done.

On a bad hand, which is rare, this print might indicate one who acts without thinking at all and can end up on the wrong side of the law because of this. Such hands are rare, fortunately.

The majority of double loops are found only on one finger—most often the index—and can add a quality of fantasy to the thinking. Thus, they can be the mark of the storyteller, the humorist, the comedian, or the actor, in whose lives this quality of fantasy can be enriching. I have seen this print on the hands of those who write songs and others who write science-fiction novels involving worlds of dragons and sorcery. It is at its best on the little fingertip and at its worst on the thumb.

Often classified as an "accidental" by law enforcement, this print is a powerful force for good on some hands, and the reverse on others.

Career possibilities if you have this print on your hand would be almost limitless, as long as they are absorbing and interesting.

They include

Puzzle writer for magazines	Environmentalist
Novelist	Astronomer
Science-fiction writer	Sculptor or model maker
Special effects technician	Naturalist
Antiques expert	Composer
Research assistant	Entertainer
Ghostwriter	Computer software investor
Historian	Comedian
Video producer	Magician
Cinematographer	

If you have chosen a career other than one of these and it is not satisfying your inner self, I would recommend that you choose one of the above as a hobby. After a time this hobby could become so successful that it will be a natural choice for a second career.

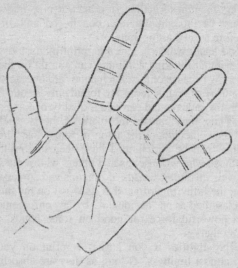

On this blank, please mark in all the various fingerprints on your dominant hand.

• • •

The importance of the fingerprints cannot be overstated in outlining potential career choices. This is why it is vital that an inked print be used to identify *exactly* which prints you possess on both hands. Looking with the naked eye at a print can result in mistaking a double loop for a peacock-feather loop, or a loop-arch for a tented loop. It may not seem all that important which is which, but in vocational analysis it can be the key to unlocking your own highest potential.

Many hand analysts not only print the entire hand, but re-ink the fingertips and print them separately at the bottom of the page to make certain they have a good, clear, and readable set. If you are not certain that you are inking the hand properly, you might wish to do the fingerprints separately. It is also important to use paper that is absorbent rather than slick or hard-surfaced. Hard or slick paper will make ink slide around, without printing clearly.

Many persons studying the hand purchase an artist's sketch-book with ring binding in which to take prints they intend to study. This paper is thick and absorbent and takes handprints very clearly when a piece of folded towel is placed behind the page. It also makes a handy, portable reference that can be studied at any time.

Fingerprints are one of the major illustrations of your own true inner self, forming perhaps 25 percent of the available knowledge and detail in any hard analysis. Classify them carefully, as they can shed much light on the path you will be traveling throughout this book.

2

SWOOPS, LOOPS, AND SWIRL PATTERNS ON THE PALM

There are often one or two of the four common loop patterns on any hand, usually between the fingers. This would be considered a normal number.

A hand with six or seven of these patterns is a most unusual one indeed. Although some have been seen.

These looping patterns on the hand are actually poolings of energies in certain known places that will outline the basic facts about your personality and temperament.

It is my feeling that the skin patterns of palm and finger are the visible reflection of the DNA genetic marker coding. Palmar lines enter between the thumb and your index finger, then sweep out, curving around the hand in a wide curve, then down and off the outside edge of the palm, or in an area at the bottom of the hand close to the wrist. Some of the eddies or changed directions they take as they sweep across the hand are vitally important as well, but a bit less common than the loop patterns themselves.

Skin Pattern Loopings

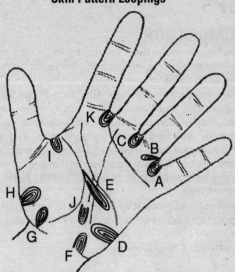

A. Humor
B. Ego (personal)
C. Common Sense
D. Ulnar

E. Memory
F. Inspiration
G. Musical or Rhythm
H. Response

I. Courage
J. Humanitarian
K. "Royal"
(Most often found in hospital study. May be inherited from one's fore-bears. Genetic.)

Some smaller loop patterns occur on the bottom sections of fingers, but these are extremely rare and therefore indicators of several most unusual personality factors.

The presence or absence of one or another of these looping patterns may give you a good deal of information about you and the career direction you should take.

LOOPS

A. HUMOR LOOP

Probably one of the most interesting loops on your hand, the humor loop marks one who can use his or her sense of humor in many areas of life.

As a rule, those who have this loop formation, large or small, possess a traditional sort of "funny bone" which reacts to jokes, funny stories, and probably sitcoms on television. This person will find humor in sight gags and the spoken words of comedians such as Johnny Carson, Jay Leno, Roseanne, Robin Williams, and many stand-up comics. Such a person enjoys comic strips, cartoons, and the latest juicy story about a celebrity.

In business, this loop may help you to keep your temper by making some humorous remark to an office mate or fellow worker.

Careerwise, it might belong to

Comedian	Military
Writer	Direct sales
Cartoonist	Telephone sales
Actor	Delivery or over-the-road
Sports	driver
Carpenter or skilled trades	Supervisor
	Receptionist

If the loop in the humor placement is very small, the sense of humor is still there but is not as broad.

See Chapter Three, "Unusual Skin Patterns," for more information on a hand that has no loop, just a right-angle formation.

If you have this loop, it may be important to discover if possible partners or marital partners have one as well, for a person with this particular formation of loop likes to interact with someone who has the same pattern on his or her hands. Since a high percentage of individuals do have a humor loop on the pad between ring and little fingers, it is usually easy to locate others who have the same marking.

This loop seems to be hereditary.

KEY WORD: ENJOYMENT

B. EGO LOOP (PERSONAL)

If the humor loop seems to be displaced to the side and is found directly under the finger, either fully rounded or somewhat flattened, then your sense of humor is different from the first sort, and you will not find fun in the same things at all.

Sharp, cutting wit, especially at the expense of others, may pull your trigger, and you will not enjoy any form of humor that could hurt someone else. Ethnic jokes, poking fun, and offbeat humor will turn you off, as will most sexual innuendo or so-called "dirty jokes."

You may find television sitcoms boring and tiresome, most newer comedians foulmouthed and irritating, and funny stories may be totally lost on you. You will have to locate your own type of humor to enjoy.

Career choices:

Social work	Historic fiction
Fund-raising	Naturalist
Stage or screen	Cinematographer
Computer	Social scientist
Journalism	Crafts

The absence of this loop does *not* mean a lack of humor, but it does illustrate how it is applied in personal and in career situations.

This sideways placement of the humor loop often marks a person who functions best in careers where he or she is solitary and in charge, or working without direct supervision by someone else.

A very large loop that dips down almost into the upper transverse or heart line may belong to someone who is enjoying life so much he or she seems to be a clown in early life, before learning to control this. If you have this enlarged loop, you are also a person who functions best in front of an audience—whether only one person or a group.

Career: Motivation seminar leader, warmup act for a show, or clown or comedian actor.

A very tiny, short loop indicates a person who has a very superficial type of humor and enjoys Martin and Lewis, Jackie Gleason and Art Carney, Abbot and Costello, and others like them. Some form of practical joke or slapstick type of humor is always being planned in his or her mind.

Career: Comedy writer, stuntman or stuntwoman, technician for special effects, or stage director for any type of comedy.

The only problem with this tiny loop is that it indicates you may be having so much fun within your own mind that you cannot see that those around you are not perceiving what's funny at all. It's best to learn tolerance for those other points of view.

In most polls regarding what each man or woman seeks in a potential mate, a sense of humor is one of the traits most often mentioned as desirable.

It is also true that the ability to laugh at oneself, if necessary, is a trait we could all put to use. If you can learn to do this, it will go a long way toward easing your pathway in life.

KEY WORD: EASYGOING

E. MEMORY LOOP

This skin pattern is often the largest on the hand, running beside or beneath the middle transverse or head line. It indicates whether or not you can remember things in general, and how well; and sometimes its length or direction can illustrate what type of things you are most likely to keep in your memory.

Obviously it would be important to discover this in any form of career aptitude analysis you might do.

If the loop appears on the hands at all, then the memory might be considered photographic, or almost perfect. Like a computer with unlimited memory storage, your mind tends to retain everything you have ever done, learned, or experienced.

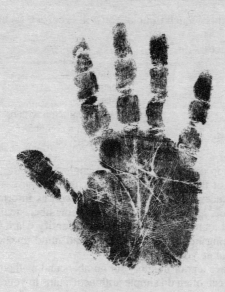

Action Hand with Long Memory Loop

All of this information is imprinted within the brain, for retrieval at some later time by the conscious mind.

For some, the sight of a certain color or the scent of a particular perfume or flower can bring up stored memories they do not know they possessed. Even a complete record of all sounds we have ever heard is stored within this mental computer so that we can often identify a piece of music from the first two or three notes or a few syllables can identify one special voice out of thousands we may have heard.

1. This loop can often be found running almost straight across the hand. In this position, it indicates that you have a good memory for facts and information. You can remember a good many telephone numbers, license plates, and where you left your keys. General information and data seem to stick in

your mind without much trouble. You will excel at tests involving memory.

Career choices:

History	Anthropology
Mathematics	Science
Writing	Sales
Teaching	Data compilation with or
Archaeology	without a computer
	Entrepreneurship

2. If the loop dips down in a slight angle toward the lower outside edge of the palm, you are more likely to have a good memory for faces, voices, and names, as well as information and experience. Like an artist, you will remember small portions of facial features, so that you could identify Clark Gable just from seeing his mustache. Games and mind puzzles are likely to fascinate you.

You will have a poor memory for numbers and mathematics, although you can often do simple arithmetic sums in your mind.

Career choices

Writing	Real estate sales
Photography	Psychology
Journalism	Art
Teaching	Piloting an airplane

NOTE: this position of the memory loop often gives you a real distaste for so-called "modern art," as the juxtapositioning of abstract concepts will trigger unpleasant feelings in your mind.

3. If the loop dips down in a sharply sloping line toward the bottom of the palm, then you are more likely to remember things best through smells, colors, shapes, and sounds.

Your memory for facts and numbers is not as good, but you can recreate entire sequences of events, even from very early childhood. As an adult, you may remember your mother's own perfume or the color of the blanket with which she covered you as a baby.

Music, sounds, and tones bring back acute memories, and your ear for music may be strong.

Career choices:

Musician, professional or amateur	Historian
Singing	Museum curator
Artist	Interior decorator
Quality control	

If there is no memory loop, it does not mean that you have no memory. It may indicate that you do not retain things as long as you would like to. You may remember a face, but not the name that goes with the face. Tests requiring memory may not be easy for you, but with concentrated study and effort, you will be able to conquer them.

As humans age, memory storage seems to ebb. In the years after fifty, we may wonder why we cannot retain facts as well as we previously did. This is a natural process of aging, but can be retarded by will, effort, and often one of the memory-assisting systems available in libraries. It is also theorized that the addition of magnesium, or foods that contain magnesium, will help naturally to improve fact retention.

If you do have a memory loop, but small and close to the middle transverse line, you might be less imaginative than you would be if the loop is long and reaches far across the palm. The ability to retain massive amounts of information seems to cut down somewhat on the ability to imagine. This is a less creative formation, but you will be a whiz at any exercise involving strictly memory.

If the loop is excessively long and drops low on the hand, the memory will supply so many pieces of information and associated factors that you may be overwhelmed by its vivid complexity.

Many artists, sculptors, fiction authors, and especially people who write for the stage have this long memory loop.

KEY WORD: RETENTION

C. COMMON SENSE LOOP

This looped marking is often found between the middle and the ring finger.

In general, if it is there at all, you will be the proud possessor of both logic and common sense. Like Mr. Spock, you will be able to assess people, information, and facts in a logical manner. This will enable you to make life choices in a reasonable manner rather than acting purely on instinct, as many people do.

This loop also brings in a factor of self-involvement, in that if the loop is small you may be prone to put the needs of others ahead of your own.

Some individuals with extremely large loops in this position will insist on having their own way about things. They will reject any and all advice and prefer to find out the results of their actions the hard way. This would be true if the loop's bottom reaches all the way to the upper transverse or head line.

This loop is a marker indicating that you possess the ability to perform straight-line thinking, without the wandering and emotional impulses that are the enemies of logical thought. You will see yourself clearly and, if you do not like what you see, will make strong efforts at making those changes that are necessary to bring yourself up to meet you own self-imposed standards.

Often the possessors of this loop are involved in continued study, such as postgraduate, and will be found in any classroom that offers them knowledge they do not presently possess.

As a student of life and living, you will put your time to good use in self-education if your hand is one of these with the common-sense loop.

Career choices include:

Doctor of medicine or chiropractic	Nursing home specialist
Social worker	Science
Medical researcher	Paralegal
Charity organizer	Emergency medicine or
Nursing	EMT
Leader of community groups	Police dispatcher
	Police or fire personnel

Whichever your field, you will be doing a good job at it, training for more skills than you already have, and you will probably have two or more absorbing hobbies as well. It is likely that you own a pc and are able to program your VCR.

KEY WORD: LOGIC

Hands that have both the humor loop and the common-sense loop on them belong to people who are well-balanced and who may spend their lives being peacemakers.

If you have both loops on your hand, you are among the fortunate. You will find that not only are people drawn to you for advice, but also you are able to give them reasonable information and counsel.

Many fine physicians, lawyers, and business leaders have this double-balanced hand.

LESS COMMON LOOPS

D. ULNAR LOOP

This loop indicates that there is a genetic or DNA characteristic that may result in an inherited problem of some sort. It is found on the lower outside edge of the hand, and may indicate only a minor problem, or perhaps something more difficult.

It has been found on the hands of Down's syndrome children, as well as persons who have inherited skeletal problems. It can indicate something as relatively minor as hay fever and allergy, or arthritis. In one hand, seen on a child of less than a year of age, it was found by physicians to indicate a lack of growth hormone, which would result in the child becoming an extremely short adult.

My finding that it referred to DNA differences has been recently confirmed by a study in Norway, where physicians located seventy different positions of this loop, and discovered the corresponding DNA problems.

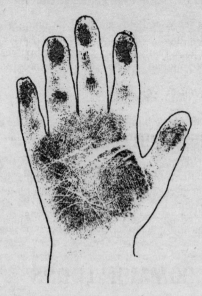

Ulnar Loop. This child is developmentally disabled, but shows extreme Artistic Ability.

It is recommended that two people who have this print on their palms undergo DNA testing before having children.

As a career factor, it is often seen on the hands of those people who love the outdoors and have a special relationship with animals. Many environmentalists have it, as do a large percentage of those called nature lovers.

Career choices:

Environmentalist
Veterinarian
Animal breeder
Animal trainer
Photographer
Park ranger

Naturalist
Animal obedience trainer or
    grooming specialist
Painter
Gardener
Landscaper
Environmental engineer

This is a most interesting pattern, with only a portion of its secrets deciphered and many mysteries yet to be decoded.

See my book *Beyond Palmistry* (Berkley, 1992) for more information about this loop.

KEY WORD: ENVIRONMENT

F. INSPIRATION LOOP

This loop is not common, and on many hands it may not even be visible unless the entire palm and wrist wrinkles are printed clearly.

It adds the quality of inspiration to the personality and indicates that you can be inspired by things that are very special to you and you alone. You may become inspired or enraptured by a certain piece of music, or by singers like Barbra Streisand and Mahalia Jackson. A good many music lovers have either this loop or some unusual skin pattern in this area of the palm.

Sometimes you may find that reading poetry or a certain book will so move you that you will memorize it and use it as a source of inspiration throughout your life.

Those with this loop often find an attraction to art or the work of a given artist, filling their walls with framed paintings or prints; or maybe a color is so attractive to you that your personal items, clothing, and home decoration will feature this color over and over again.

In addition to this aspect, those who possess this loop seem to have the ability to draw to them others who love the same things.

One woman who has this marking has become so fond of the work of a certain artist that she has filled her home with his paintings and written several books on them.

Such a person may be a natural leader, a crusader, even a religiously inspired speaker like Billy Graham, Dr. Norman Vincent Peale, or Martin Luther King.

Either a loop or a distinctive pattern in this area may mark such charismatic individuals as Oprah Winfrey, Johnny Cash,

Bill Cosby, or any naturally charming and attractive people who draw crowds and loyal followings without effort.

Such people are inspired and often inspiring, and if your hand has either the loop or a distinctive skin pattern in this area, consider yourself lucky indeed!

Career choices:

Minister, priest, or evangelist	Educator
Artist	Greeting card designer
Color therapist	Sports leader or coach
Art curator or collector	Politics
Poet	Charity organizer
Author	Motivational speaker
Teacher	

Emotion and intellect work equally for those who possess this fascinating and rare skin pattern.

KEY WORD: INSPIRATION

G. MUSICAL OR RHYTHM LOOP

If this loop appears on the base of the hand, the person is in some way sensitive to rhythm or to music. It may be only a love for listening to music that has a definite, noticeable rhythmic beat, or the music may be used to coordinate with motion. Many dancers have this loop, as do figure skaters like Brian Boitano and Nancy Kerrigan.

Oddly, it is also found on the hands of sports figures, who find their natural body rhythm aids them in their chosen sports performance. Although it might not be noticeable at first, there is some definite coordination and rhythmic quality to a champion (or a fine amateur) skier, skater, surfer, tennis player, or golfer that directs their timing and performance ability.

Most persons who have this loop will find it just below the rings around the base of the thumb, although it might be hard to see due to the usual fine lines in this area that are not part of the skin pattern itself.

If you believe you have this loop on your hand, run your

index finger down the outside edge of the thumb. If you feel a bump just below the thumb, indicating an enlargement of this hidden knuckle, you have the loop, no matter how small. This bump also indicates that you have a temper, so you should take steps to control this personality aspect as soon as you recognize it. I have seen great sports personalities lose their temper and pitch a golf club or a baseball bat away without looking to see if anyone was in its path. I'm sure you've seen this kind of thing as well.

Anger can be a cleansing force to remove frustration, or it can be a destructive force when used without thought.

Career choices:

Sports	Athletic coach
Dancer	Olympic trainer
Choreographer for stage or screen	Ballroom dancer
Musician	Actor
Composer	Musical comedy
Athlete	Swimmer, driver, gymnast

If you have this loop, you should find a way to use your natural body rhythm to its best advantage. It is never too late to begin a new career, even in sports, and even if it must remain a hobby rather than a paying job. It can and does relate to a natural talent you possess and were born with. It is up to you to find how best to utilize this talent.

KEY WORD: GRACE

H. RESPONSE LOOP

Slightly higher on the thumb and sometimes even more difficult to see, the response loop belongs to those who are strongly and naturally affected by people around them and by events in their lives.

It might be nearly invisible due to secondary lines of the area near the thumb, but with strong magnification it is visible, but only on 4 percent of human hands. These are frequently of

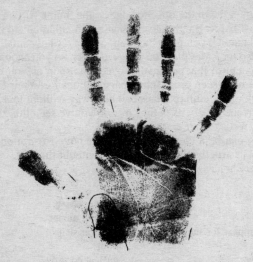

A

This hand shows the rare response loop. Print A is the hand at age fifteen. Print B is the same woman at age thirty-three. There have been major changes in the lines, and the hand now resembles the action type—a rare occurrence initiated by complete change of life circumstances, including divorce, remarriage, and a new and satisfying career as a chef. Her humor loop kept her stable, for it is a large one.

Mediterranean heritage—for instance, Italy, Greece, Cypriot, Turkey, Arabia, and Egypt. If your own ancestors came from these areas, it is likely that you have this loop on one of your hands.

Persons who have this loop are keenly sensitive to those around them, to their surroundings, to beautiful sunsets, sunrises, weather fronts or barometric changes, and most of all the people who are closest to them.

Many who have this loop, or a raised bump in the indicated area, are emotionally changeable. They have a chameleonlike quality, for if they are with negative persons, they become negative, while positive groups bring out the best in them.

If you have this loop, you will be quite earnest and concen-

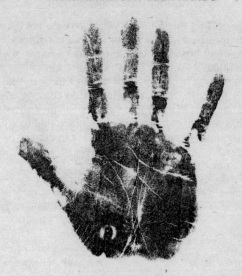

B

trate on your work or listen closely to the directions of your superiors when you find yourself in a group or an office that is quiet and serious. If the group is in a party mood, or a careless, slapdash attitude prevails, you may find it very difficult to keep from joining in. It is very important that you try to discover a group of positively motivated, goal-oriented individuals with whom to live or to work. Avoid negative persons or "losers," for they can pull you down with them.

If you cannot see this loop even under magnification, run your fingertip over the area, and you may find a projecting bump that should be regarded as almost as strong an indication.

If you have either the loop or the bump, you should be careful of your physical surroundings also, keeping them full of color and light. There is a slight claustrophobia in people with this loop, and you should be aware that you may become extremely uncomfortable in a confined, closed-in space like a jail, submarine, or small elevator. Darkness may also affect you, it is best to keep some or all work and play areas well lit in the winter.

If you do find this loop on your hand, do not consider it a threatening aspect, for it is not, unless conditions exist that make you feel boxed in, unable to make a move or change in your situation.

For those whose employment requires them to deal with the public or to speak, teach, act, sing, or do comedy, it is a good thing to have this loop for these people can then almost feel the mood and response of the audience, since this loop is almost always associated with sympathy and with empathy.

Careers:

Psychologist	Novelist
Employment counselor	Biographer
Instructor or teacher	Social work, as long as it is
Performer	positive in nature
Comedian	Songwriter
Acting coach	Hypnotherapist
Writer, scriptwriter	Osteopath or homeopath

If you have this loop, you may find that you have an almost psychic quality, as you will often know what people are about to say or do, and you are sensitive and responsive to the moods and feelings of mates, children, or relatives.

This loop has negatives, but if you learn how to keep your inner self positive, it can be a huge asset.

KEY WORD: SENSITIVITY

I. COURAGE LOOP

Theoretically, it might seem that a loop by this name would be found more often on the hands of men, the natural gladiators. I have seen it on the hands of women as well, however.

These are people who possess not only a daring try-any-thing-once sort of attitude, but also a logical, realistic attitude toward life and death. It is not the mark of the foolishly brave, but that of those who will scale cliffs or descend into caves to rescue another person in trouble.

For this reason, it may be the special symbol of most paramedics, disaster teams, and people whose job it is to excel in giving physical aid to those in need.

Even if the loop is not complete, there may be some twist or bend in the normally even-flowing skin pattern between thumb and index finger that will give away its presence, and you can look more closely to locate it.

Career choices:

Paramedic	Toxic chemical expert
Ambulance technician	Oil well fire specialist
S.W.A.T. team	Ski instructor
Drug enforcement agent	Mountain rescue team
Emergency room nurse or doctor	Fireman
Athlete	Police, sheriff's department,
Fire jumper	etc.
	Stuntman or stuntwoman

Obviously, I have had to eliminate many other categories here where the loop could be supportive, if not a major career factor. If you have this loop, you may be wondering where I am coming from, as you are not a James Bond type. But there will be an aspect of courage and leadership within you that makes you a natural leader, an innovator, an inventive, and resource-ful person. You may have expressed this by joining your local school board, becoming a volunteer for a political party or candidate of your choice, leading a Girl Scout or Boy Scout troop, or any of the modern-day problem-solving teams that require courage and adaptability.

Sometimes in today's world it takes these qualities just to be a good parent!

Often classroom mischief-makers, either male or female, those who have this loop or pattern disruption grow up to be among the most helpful and responsive of adults.

If you do not have this formation, but there is a congregation of secondary skin lines in this area overlying the skin pattern, it will signify that although not born with these abilities, you have had to acquire them as you went. This is one of the things I admire most about human nature: the ability of an "ordinary" man or woman leading an ordinary life, to come through when

Some Skin Loop Patterns

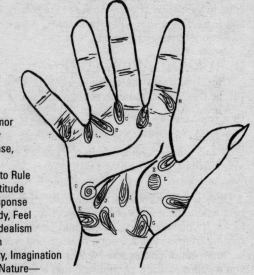

A. Sense of Humor
B. Ego or Vanity
C. Common Sense, Strength
D. Power, Born to Rule
E. Courage, Fortitude
F. Sense of Response
G. Music, Melody, Feel
H. Inspiration, Idealism
I. Humanitarian
J. Good Memory, Imagination
K. Affinity with Nature— the Ulnar Loop
L. Musical Genius, Composer, Artist
M. Charisma, Presence
N. Ultra-Femininity or Masculinity
O. Intensity, Exaggeration

the need arises, such as during a natural disaster fire, or highway accident—turning into the brave, no-thought-for-self rescuer!

Recently an airplane crashed beside a busy highway. Many drivers sped by, oblivious (or afraid), yet other cars and trucks stopped, and people ran toward the aircraft to drag out the occupants who were trapped inside the burning wreckage. Though not super heroes, they possessed the finer stuff of which real leaders are made.

Should this marking appear on your hand, you may not feel that you have ever utilized the courage or fortitude it reveals, but sometime, somewhere in your lifetime you *will* use it. It may not be your career, but could be your destiny!

KEY WORD: BRAVERY

J. HUMANITARIAN LOOP

Closely akin to the courage loop, this one can be found on the hands of persons in organizations like the Sierra Club or Greenpeace, doing their level best for humanity and the planet.

It might also be found on the hands of seemingly ordinary men and women who are "geared" to seek out the best in others. When people who have this loop are still young, they often have a tendency to see others through rose-colored glasses. Then they find through life experience that many idols, stars, or leaders have seamy pasts or private lives, and disillusionment and depression may set in. This can result in a wiser person with more insight.

If the other personality factors indicated on the hand are strong and well balanced, this loop might belong to an idealist, a person who works in his or her own way for peace and the well-being of all humans. On a weaker hand the loop might indicate a cynical, embittered misfit whose illusions about human nature lie in ruins.

Sometimes the humanitarian loop appears on the hands of crusading journalists who spend their time uncovering scandals: sometimes on those persons who feel it their mission to expose people whom they believe to be charlatans. The danger here is that they may be blaming the innocent due to one individual who created antagonism in their minds. An example of this might be the individual who feels all ministers or evangelists are money-grubbing fakes, because he or she was taken by one, while ignoring the fact that many of these persons are honest and trustworthy. Or a person with this loop may feel he or she has a right to crusade against all psychics, since in the past he or she has encountered one who was dishonest.

But the nature of this skin pattern is basically that of a person who is geared to find the best in others, not the worst.

Career Choices:

Counselor	Image consultant
Teacher	Jury consultant
Motivation seminar leader	Constitutional law specialist
Inspirational writer or speaker	Government
Journalist	

If this loop appears on your hand, or if there's any disruption in the skin pattern in this place, it might serve you well to study motivational psychology and the teachings of Napoleon Hill and Dr. Norman Vincent Peale for enlightenment and enrichment without trading your natural positive nature for negativism.

KEY WORD: IDEALISTIC

"ROYAL" LOOP

Seldom seen on any hand, this is one of the two definitely DNA-related loopings. When I first encountered it, it was being heralded as something found only on the hands of persons descended from royalty.

As I began to really study hands, however, and to apply for perhaps the first time some real common sense to this study, it became apparent to me that royalty is not a hereditary factor, passed on in the bloodlines. Often people entirely unrelated to any previous kings, emperors, or rulers are by chance catapulted into the position of ruling a country. One good example would be the Napoleonic Marshal, Jean Bernadotte, who was chosen by a faraway Scandanavian country to become its king. Another might be the case of Alexander the Great, upon whose death all of his generals took over and became kings in those countries where they had been appointed governors by Alexander. In this way, Cleopatra, daughter of Ptolemy, became queen of Egypt. The original Ptolemy had merely been one of Alexander's generals. So how could Ptolemy's sudden rise to pharaoh have marked his skin patterns, which had been on his hand all of his life?

Obviously, something was wrong with that interpretation.

Later it was reported that the loop was most often found on the hands of individuals who were in mental hospitals, thus leading to the idea that all who had it on their hands must be one step from the psychiatrist and the straitjacket.

There was something wrong with that idea, too.

What may be true is that the loop is sometimes found on the hands of persons who possess chromosomal abnormalities.

It is also true that those who have this loop often have very strong, even overpowering, personalities, and this may be why it was assigned such an unusual distinction.

Recently this loop was located on the hands of a young woman in California, a specialist in juvenile law, and who stated to me that she was working hard toward being a judge specializing in youth and juvenile cases.

Other individuals who have had it were also involved in assisting others, perhaps not as a jurist, but as a school counselor. Others have been actors, especially those who do their acting on a stage, where presence and power and personality projection are definite assets.

It would be hard to say what careers would be indicated for those with this loop, but perhaps the above will be helpful as guidelines.

Career Choices: actor, debater, public speaker, jurist, and specialist in juvenile legal problems.

As hand analysis is not a finite science, but an ongoing study of the specifics of human characteristics, I would like to encourage you, if you have this loop between your index and middle fingers on either hand, to make a good clear print and send it to me, along with information about what you have chosen as a career, or what career you would choose if you were free to do so.

You may send it to the address in the About the Author section of this book.

KEY WORD: CHARITABLE

UNFINISHED LOOPS

As I have stated in several places, the placement of the loop formation is most important, not the presence of the loop.

In each of the places you may find not a loop, but a half loop—a right-angle bending of the skin pattern. In a career sense, this has the same meaning as a complete loop.

There was one such incomplete loop on the hand of the great psychoanalyst and pioneer psychiatrist Carl Jung. It was in the location of the humor loop, but was not a complete formation. Thus, it could have indicated that his sense of humor was unusual, offbeat, or may have not developed at all. From what we know of him, however, he seems to have been blessed with a normal sense of humor.

Another individual whose print I investigated recently had a partial memory loop. He admitted to being able to recall and hear entire musical selections in his inner ear, which is a feat of memory not possessed by many. Some singers, specifically the great Barbra Streisand, have the ability not only to carry entire complex melodies in their memories, but also to compose music themselves, which is no small accomplishment!

If you have an unfinished or partial loop on your own hand, you should consider it to be a loop and consider the same career aptitudes and skills as those attributed to loops above. You might, however, consider that the half-loop may not be quite as influential as if it were complete.

All formations on the hand that are not just the swooping curves of the basic skin pattern can be considered important, whether a loop or not, and they should be given their meanings based on the place in which they appear more than the shape they take. Basic patterns may curve but never loop completely.

PALMAR SECTIONS

These skin loops are found in areas of the hand that will correspond to specific portions of the human psychological makeup.

Loops spotlight certain kinds of responses. If a loop is NOT present between the ring and middle fingers, for instance, it does not indicate that you have no common sense, but that some other area of your personality is stronger or more distinctive.

A. Amusement:	This small segment of the hand refers to your ability to enjoy life. The loop would indicate a stronger form of humorous expression.
B. Analytical Mind:	This inter-finger area indicates the ability to analyze and assess the environment and events that may involve or interest us.
C. Memory Bank:	This large area of the palm is devoted to how and what we remember and store in our subconscious memory bank.
D. Adventure:	This sizeable section of the palm refers to how we handle risks, danger, and challenges.
E. Music:	Embedded in the third section of the thumb, our enjoyment of music can be an important part of life.
F. Absorption:	The ability to relate and interrelate our feelings and responses with those around us is the province of this small palm segment.
G. Genetic:	This section of the lower palm may contain a loop or other marking that reveals something about our genetic code. It is also the area for allergies, indicating that they may be inherited.
H. Idealistic:	This basal section reflects the part of us that is not only capable of becoming inspired, but also idealistic in nature.
I. Charismatic:	This area of the hand reflects our ability to draw others to us as well as our talent for making a lasting impression on those with whom we live and work.

Skin Pattern Loopings

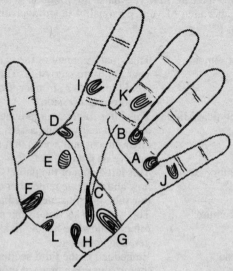

A. Amusement   E. Music   I. Charismatic
B. Analytical Mind   F. Absorption   J. Intensity
C. Memory Bank   G. Genetic   K. Ownership
D. Adventurer   H. Idealism   L. Timing

These areas of the hand refer to certain psychological human factors. A
loop or other unusual skin marking may appear in these areas. They
might also be puffed as if inflated with an air bubble.

J. Intensity: Small but significant, this section of the
                       hand indicates the quality of our inten-
                       sity as well as our sexual quotient.
K. Ownership: This area of the palmar surface often
                       reveals our desire and ability to hold on
                       to what we have, as well as our need to
                       acquire new possessions.

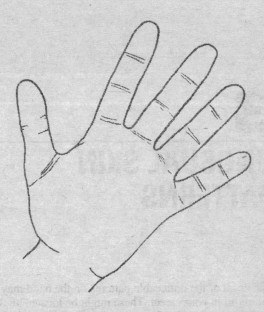

On this blank, please sketch in the looped patterns you find on your dominant hand.

L. Timing: This small area toward the middle of the palmar bottom refers to our sense of timing and rhythmic motion, even to dancing ability.

These areas may have no loop or other specialized <u>marking</u>, but may be puffed up in appearance, having almost the same quality as a loop.

3

UNUSUAL SKIN PATTERNS

Some or all of the noticeable patterns on the hand may also be meaningful in your career. These might be located on the palm or infrequently on the fingers' lower sections. I have not personally seen one on a middle phalange (finger section), but it is possible that they exist. I would appreciate receiving a print of a hand with such a marking.

FINGER-SECTION LOOPS

F. THE CHARISMA LOOP

A loop on the lowest section of the index finger will indicate a personality that is almost magnetic in intensity. The person has the ability to draw others as friends and associates.

The loop is uncommon, but it might be found on the hands of great statesmen, leaders who have the ability to inspire others. Even people with strong personalities themselves are

56

Unusual Skin Patterns

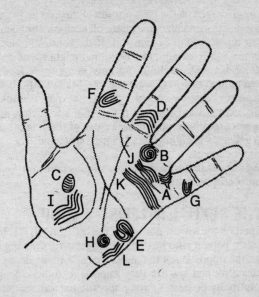

often drawn as if by an invisible magnet to such charismatic leaders.

Men and women will follow such a person, even if the direction in which he or she is heading is not the best for their own purposes. Some religious leaders may have had this marking, and it was found on the hands of Mahatma Gandhi, John F. Kennedy, and John Wayne.

Possible career choices:

Owning a business	Lawyer, judge
Stage, screen, television	Metaphysician
Minister, priest, rabbi	Teacher
Politician	

D. THE POSSESSIONS LOOP

A loop located on the base portion of the middle finger marks an individual who can concentrate on accumulating land, property, or a collection of some sort. If the tip of the index finger bends in slightly as well, the individual might spend most or all of his or her time seeking out new items to collect. Among those who had this loop were the late Malcolm Forbes, Jackie Gleason, and eclectic collector and artist Andy Warhol.

This skin pattern formation may not completely loop, but will sometimes hump up in the center of the finger section. If so, it indicates a slightly less intense individual.

Career choices:

Real estate, museum curator, antiques collector and dealer, or corporation executive.

G. THE SEXUAL INTENSITY LOOP

Found on the lowest portion of the little finger, this loop will indicate a person who has sexual magnetism, drawing individuals of the opposite sex to themselves as a flame draws a moth.

Sensuality and sex are very important to these people, and they normally possess a strong appetite for romance and physical love.

To have this loop on the little finger is an unusual thing, and it might be either an asset or a handicap. Unless the owner can fulfill the intense urges of his or her deep inner nature and find close and deep relationships in romance and marriage, he or she may become a miserably unhappy person.

One might suspect this loop to have been on the hands of such great stars as Errol Flynn, Clark Gable, and Marilyn Monroe, but it has been seen on less flamboyantly sensual persons as well.

Some career options that would make use of this unusual skin pattern might be:

Model, actor/actress, designer, musician/orchestra/band leader, or singer.

THE SOCIABILITY LOOP

Rarest of all the loops, this one if located on the base section of the ring finger, and marks a personality that is in its element when surrounded with groups of friends and associates. Party-loving, these people love to spend a great deal of time communicating with friends and family.

(Just as a joke, one of my early hand analysis classes chose to call a long, slim little finger the "telephone finger," as it was most often used to dial a phone, but this will be accentuated if there is an unusual loop or odd pattern found on the base of the ring finger as well.) Communication is this person's best suit, and his or her career should involve one or another of the many varieties of making contact with others.

Careers:

Sales work	Social director for travel
Promotional work	agency or cruise ships
Public relations	Director for stage, screen, or
Advertising	TV
Dancer, gymnast	Team sports
	Telephone sales work

Any unusual formation on this finger segment will mark a person who loves cruises, tours, meeting and associations of all types, and who will work hard in groups or committees within political organizations, the PTA, or the Masonic Order.

Such people often possess a sense of drama also. This loop appeared on the hands of such notables as Lady Sarah Churchill, Victor Mature, and Bela Lugosi of Dracula fame. The great psychologist/psychiatrist Carl Jung was known to have an unusual pattern on this finger section.

J. THE ELECTRONIC "WAVE"

Often there is a noticeably upward-curving skin pattern formation running just beneath the ring and little fingers, above the upper transverse or heart line.

This is known as the "electronics" or "electrical" formation,

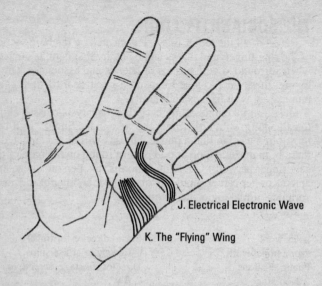

J. Electrical Electronic Wave

K. The "Flying" Wing

and belongs to people who have a natural affinity for these two fields. In the past, at a time when women were not involved in either of these fields, a hand analyst would suggest that a woman with this was marking the type of homemaker who could rewire an electric lamp or replace a burned-out tube in the television set. Today the "wave" might be found on the hands of a female electrician, electrical engineer, or telephone line person.

Careers:

Anything that involves wires, circuitry, gadgetry; electrical or electronics work; computer programmer; computer repair; and engineering.

K. THE "FLYING" WING

This pattern belongs to those who have a positive love for flying, or a hate or fear of flying.

It is found on the hands of many who have taken lessons to learn to fly an airplane, as well as on the hands of people of all ages who wish they had had the chance to learn.

Oddly, it marks not only the person who will take an airplane anytime, anywhere, but also members of the "white knuckle club," who tense up apprehensively at the very thought of flying in an aircraft.

If you have this marking, you may be well fitted in talent and inclination, for a job as a travel agent or a tour guide, but if you are a member of the airplane-hating group, you may be better off taking a job as a map cartographer in a nice warm library somewhere.

Bearers of this skin pattern are also acutely sensitive to air currents, and either like all doors and windows securely shut, or all windows open and a fan blowing on them as they sleep.

B. THE PRACTICALITY WHORL

Not often seen, this circular marking might take the place of the common sense loop on some hands. It marks the person who is essentially so well organized and practical that he or she makes others feel disorganized by comparison.

All whorl patterns on fingers or palm mark intensity, and the area between the ring and middle fingers is the area of self-education, common sense, and practicality. The whorl indicates an individual who has these talents to an excessive degree.

Career choices:

Accountant	Environmental engineer
Janitorial services agency	CPA, Accountant, IRS agent
Statistician	Constitutional lawyer
Safety engineer	Paralegal

A. THE REVERSE L FORMATION

This marking indicates that the owner has an acutely dry sense of humor, or prefers absurdities or wit to all other forms of comedy, such as slapstick. If you have this marking, you may prefer a humorous story to any type of joke. You may get angry rather than laugh at persons pulling practical jokes, and you would probably be bored stiff watching *America's Funniest Home Videos* but laugh hysterically at a blooper or an odd newspaper headline or misprint. Pratfalls and custard pies in the face are not your cup of tea.

Career choices:

Newspaper columnist	Midwife
Writer	Advertising agency
Emergency medicine	Insurance agent
Paramedic	

C. THE MUSICAL "BEE"

This formation actually *looks* like the back end of a honey-bee, a rounded oval with stripes of skin patterning within the outline.

It is not uncommon, and if you find one on your hand, you are either the kind of person who must have music playing in the background most of the time, or you may be performing it yourself in public or private.

This mark does not belong to the bathtub tenor, but to the person who is drawn to music as a major form of expression.

If it is combined with a very long tip on the little finger, you may be a person who writes your own songs, or even composes music of one kind of another.

If a child is seen to have this on his or her hand, early training should be given in either playing an instrument or using the voice. It is probably most important of all that the child be taught to *read* music.

If you find this bee on your hand and you are not at an age when formal or costly training is feasible, remember that inexpensive keyboards are available in almost any discount store and in most malls, as are other instruments and books on how to play them. It is not necessary to own a Steinway or a Yamaha to play music.

This hand contains the musical "bee" formation (circled), the ulnar loop, the common-sense loop, and the healing stigmata. The owner is a thirty-six-year-old psychiatric nurse who plays classical piano for her own amusement and in concerts. The drooping head line shows a tendency to depression, which can be alleviated by listening to music.

Possible careers:

Musician
Composer
Pianist, guitarist, etc.
Singer

Writer of musical comedies
Amateur theatricals involving music
Music teacher
Music store owner or employee

If singing is your first love, you should be able to find an amateur or semi-professional group such as a barbershop quartet. This can become a fine hobby and provide much enjoyment for yourself as well as for others, even if it is only a hobby and not a full-time career!

If you have *any* unusual formation in this area, it will indicate that you should be involved with music, and it would behoove you to get started as soon as possible.

I. THE DRAMATIC ARCH

This formation is quite common and marks the individual who is essentially involved in "finding" him- or herself. It usually indicates a person who is independent and not too closely tied to family.

Self-expression is the most urgent need of persons with this skin pattern, and if you have it you should devote yourself to discovering all you can about yourself, what makes you "tick."

You are a person of strong desires and appetites and usually try to enjoy life to its fullest. Although you feel you do not need other people to complete your life, you must remember that even the sun needs something to reflect its light, or it would shine alone, all show and no substance. For this reason you should seek friends and associates who are compatible with you. In marriage you must learn to be a giver as well as a taker.

There are only four or five skin patterns found within the semicircle known as the lifeline, and because of this they are of extreme importance in any analysis of the hand.

Possible career choices:

Actor, actress	Professional athlete
Chef or restaurateur	Casino dealer, pit boss, cashier
Naturalist	Pharmacist
Environmentalist	Artist
Cinematographer	Park ranger
Theologian	Photographer
Professional researcher	Private detective
Author	

H. THE IMAGINATION WHORL

If this skin pattern appears on your hand, you have a truly wild imagination! You may be a writer, storyteller, artist, actor or actress, or all of these together!

Hands with this marking often belong to avid fans of science fiction such as *Star Wars* and *Star Trek*. If you have this marking, space and the universe fascinate you. You love puzzles and mysteries and will climb a volcano just to see what the inside looks like, or keep a large file of magazines on unusual subjects if you are unable to travel.

You will dress distinctively, wear unusual jewelry, and usually will completely disregard whatever is in fashion to wear your own particular style of clothing and accessories.

If you have this mark, not only your mind is unusual, but also your hobbies, your friends, and even your home and your automobile. You will make your own way and glory in it.

Careers:

Writer, poet	Hair or cosmetic stylist
Science fiction	Clothing or fabric design
Archaeologist	Paleontologist
Astronomer	Egyptologist
Planetarium worker	Entrepreneur
Aeronautical engineer	Inventor
Designer	
Actor, actress	

E. THE NATURE DOUBLE LOOP

This marking is rare and unusual, but is found on the hands of persons who have a deep and abiding love for the outdoors, and for nature in general.

Often selfless for one reason or another, they spend their lives as caretakers for the world, protecting it from the rest of us.

If this marking appears on your hand, you are best suited to a career that allows you lots of out-of-doors time and some access to or contact with plants, trees, mountains, lakes, fresh air, and lots and lots of sunshine.

This mark also tends to make the owner draw into him or herself. This person is able to remember what is seen and heard so acutely that whole symphonies can be replayed in the mind, or the exact colors of a roomful of tropical orchids can be recalled.

If you have this loop, it is important that you find some career in which you can feel useful, accomplishing something and not just wasting your time.

Careers:

Botanist	Landscaper
Flower arranger	Park ranger
Gardener	Naturalist
Conservationist	Astronomer
Artist	Meteorologist, weather
Woodcarver	researcher

L. THE DREAMER'S ARCH

If you have this unusual formation on your hand, you are a person who dreams vividly and in color. You may also be a daydreamer and possibly an idealist.

This marking also indicates strong intuition, and some of your dreams and experiences may be precognitive or psychic.

You are moved by beauty, sunsets, sunrises, scenery, flowers, birds, and butterflies. Music may also have a strong effect on your state of mind, and harsh, discordant music may actually upset you or infuriate you.

In this particular portion of the hand, which represents the inner mind and imagination, the arch has particular strength.

If there is a deep dimple or dent in this place, it marks the person who has the ability to sense what others are thinking or what they are about to say. If the skin pattern is found in conjunction with the dent or dimple, then this aspect is even stronger.

Possible career choices:

Artist	Psychologist
Musician	Writer, poet
Fabric designer	Marriage counselor
Inventor	Social worker
Priest, nun, minister	Pediatrician

Until the research my group and I began in the early 1960s, there had been *no* notice taken of these distinctive and fascinating skin patterns on the hand. Yet, with just these alone, a fairly complete and complex psychological analysis can be done of any hand. Careerwise, it is best to cross-check all of the observed patterns in a hand and find a career that is related to the most mentioned fields. It may be that several of your own skin patterns lead to the same career direction. If any two or more of them can be related in this way, this will be the best choice of fields for you, and you can manage to find a niche in this area.

If several are indicated, then it might be that one set will outline career direction, while the rest may be rewarding or profitable hobbies.

There is *no* hand that does not have two or more of these unusual skin patterns. Yet there is so much more to discover.

4

HAND SIZES AND SHAPES

RIGHT BRAIN/LEFT BRAIN

The fact that the left and right sides of the human brain have definite differences between them has only been explored by science in the past several decades. The right brain commands the artistic, intuitive, imaginitive part of our personalities, while the left brain operates more on logic and experiential processes.

This discovery answered an ancient question about visible differences between right and left hands. Traditionally the left hand was thought to be the one that exhibited your inherited traits, while the right hand showed what you had done with these factors.

When the right-and left-brain differential was outlined, it quickly became apparent that the reason your hands are different is that the two sides of your brain are different. Since the right brain controls the left hand, this (generally) nondominant hand will exhibit some of the contents of the creative and artistic side of your personality makeup. This area would be of intense assistance in a career that involves having to be creative or to come up with new solutions, such as desktop publishing, design, or window display.

The right hand will reflect the left-brain areas of logical thinking, and experiences that have changed and molded your outward-oriented personality and your take-charge abilities, another strong factor in career analysis.

Skin patterns appear on both hands, along with the patterns we have been covering in the last two chapters, if a complete analysis is to be done, both sets of data should be considered.

You might think of the right hand as your conscious mind, and the left hand as the other half of you, the subconscious. It takes both portions of the mind to supply you with the ability to participate in day-to-day activities, and long-term planning, creativity, and memory. Of course, if you are left-dominant, simply reverse all of the following functions. Your left hand then becomes the dominant one. This will be true of all right- and left-brain differences.

The functions of the two hands are as follows:

Right hand (conscious level):

Awake	Making connections consciously
Alert	Making decisions
Seeing	Reacting to stimulus
Hearing	Gathering information
Touching	Impulsive behavior
Tasting	Learning new things
Experiencing	Sexual attraction
Reacting	All forms of perception
Smelling	Logical thought processes

Left hand (subconscious mind):

Making connections,	Love
intuitively learned behaviors	Instinctual behavior
Remembering	Supplying learned information

Sorting information	Storing data
Intuitive thoughts	Deeper emotions
Creative processes	Conscience
Wondering	Imagining
Recognizing	

Like a computer, your conscious mind receives data and information you gain through daily experience, and your subconscious mind stores this for future use.

Psychologists theorize that there is a third area of mind, the superconscious, that is our real conscience and the abode of our spiritual nature.

In this area of mind are such higher impulses as nurturing, self-sacrifice, and the process of becoming civilized. Inspiration and our connection to our creator also belong to this higher level, which acts as our guiding force.

In this area of mind also arise the hunches, gut feelings, and deep intuitive wisdom that are called psychic.

Hand analysts gather information on this higher aspect of mankind through the length, strength, and condition of the middle fingers on both right and left hands.

The dominant hand supplies information about what is going on in the life at present and in the recent past, although even long past events are indicated on the hand as well.

It should be remembered that hand analysis is not fortune-telling, for, like a tape recorder, the hand can only record what has happened and what *is* happening. If it has not yet happened, it cannot be recorded on the hand.

Since everything about the hand changes constantly throughout life, no long-term information about the future can be gained from it. It is possible to spot trends and directions in a hand, however, so that a projection can be made about what path a person will follow as a career, as well as in other areas, such as physical health. Present trends and events, then, foreshadow the future *possibilities*. Palmists often mistake these trends for certainties, not realizing that a change in lifestyle will also change the lines on the hand.

The lines on the nondominant or subconscious hand usually change much more slowly than those on the dominant hand. The only thing that never changes on either hand is the skin patterning itself. Comparing a print taken of your hand at birth with a current one will show great changes in the lines and their placement, but never a change in the skin patterns.

THE FOUR TYPES OF HANDS

In my first book, *Beyond Palmistry*, the four basic shapes of hands and fingers were described as geared to the four personality types.

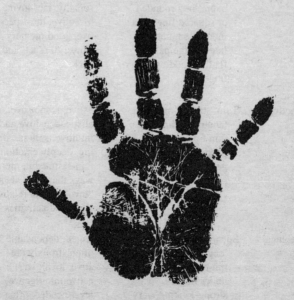

Action Hand

Rounded, curved palm, widespread shortish round fingers, slim nails, thumb, and little finger at wide angle. Warm, firm, well-padded hand.

In career diagnosis, it is not as important to recognize the blendings of the four types, but it is important to categorize your basic hand shape as one of the four major shapes.

These shapes are:

Action:	Rounded palm, high padding under fingers; short fingers, usually widespread; moderate number of lines on the palm.	Fast-thinking and fast-moving, restless, alert, creative, warmhearted, open, emotional, dominant generous, perceptive
Mental:	Oblong or rectangular palm, long rounded or squared fingers, a moderate number of lines on the palm, flattish padding under fingers	Thinkers, cognitive personality, fact-loving, inventive, introspective, good memory, slower to react, laid back
Emotional:	Thin, straight-sided rectangular palm, long thin fingers, thin padding under fingers, many lines on palm	Creative, responsive, idealistic, sensitive and intuitive, self-sacrificing, deeply emotional, thin-skinned in more ways than one, always "involved" in relationships and activities
Technical:	Squared palm, medium-length fingers, medium-high padding under fingers, very strong-looking, very few lines on palm	Talented, dependable often strongly creative, loyal, with active intelligence, level-headed, often shy or withdrawn but blooms when given love and friendship

Most hands will fall into one of these main categories. Even within a family there may be persons with all or most of these basic human types.

It is possible, but rare, to find two completely different types and sizes of hand on the same individual; talk show host and comedian Jay Leno's hands are very different in size and finger shapes. This may be a visible difference as in his case, or a subtle one that is revealed when both hands are printed.

To summarize:

Action hand: energetic, achieving, perceptive
Mental hand: thoughtful, creative, intellectual
Emotional hand: sensitive, loving, reactive
Technical hand: trustworthy, successful, broad-minded

• • •

Mental Hand

Rectangular hand, long fingers with smooth or squared sides. Fingers may have round or squared-off tips. Moderate number of lines. Warm, soft skin.

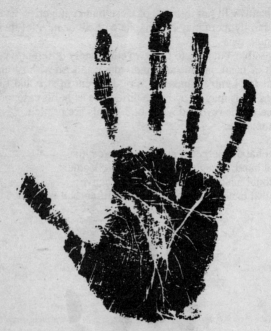

Emotional Hand

Long hand, slim to thin, rectangular shape, with prominent knuckles and thin thumb. Many lines make skin look wrinkled. Skin usually soft, cool, and dry. May have loose skin between fingers.

In general, the wide hand belongs to the doer, the achiever, those who are involved in active careers, hobbies, and projects that will usually end in success.

Although it was believed for some time that long, narrow hands were the mark of intellect and talent, it is now obvious that this supposition was in error, and that all four hand shapes indicate their own areas of creativity and intelligence. Wider hands are capable of achievement in specializations from medicine to engineering. And people with these hands possess the energy and strength that some of their narrow-handed neighbors lack.

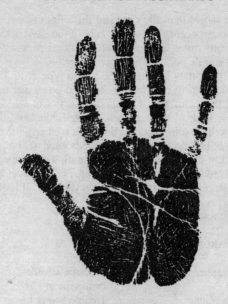

Technical Hand

Square palm; strong, rounded, or squared-off fingers. Wide nails, fingers closer together. Low-set thumb that may have an angular base. Warm, hard, flattish palm; thick, smooth skin.

WIDE HANDS

This hand is strong-looking, usually is rounded or massively square in the palm, with powerful, rounded fingers, flattish fingernails, and a warm, slightly dry, and rough texture. In a print of this hand there will not be a multiplicity of lines.

This hand normally has a longer index finger than ring finger. The length of the middle finger is not as important as the length of the two fingers that flank it.

In most of these hands, the majority of the palmar lines will be found on the side toward the thumb. If a line were drawn up the center of the palm, from the wrist to the tip of the middle finger, you would find that the index finger and thumb were somewhat larger than the ring and little fingers, even in their width. This is because the thumb side of the hand is the area of the conscious mind, and most wide-handed persons use their conscious minds very actively in all they do.

These hands may belong to the action type or to the technical type, depending on whether the hand possesses the roundedness of the palm and widespread fingers of action, or the squared-off look of the technical hand. Finger length will be short to medium long, and there will be a clearly rounded area between each of the fingers. Wide hands need not be large, and in fact action hands are often quite small. They are most easily recognized by their widespread fingers. Technical hands are often the largest of all hands and have a powerful look even in repose.

Career choices:

ACTION HANDS

Detective
Cinematographer
Tour guide
Convention planner
Psychologist
Metaphysician

Writer
Research science
Paramedic or EMT
Troubleshooter
Owning own business
Archaeology
Paleontology
Reporter
Investigative reporter

TECHNICAL HANDS

Journalist
Private detective
Conservation
Gardener/landscaper
Teacher
Printer
Pianist
Musician/composer
Professional sports
Cook/chef

Metalworking
Building contractor
Jeweler/watchmaker
Surgeon
Emergency medicine
Electronics
Computer science
Lawyer or judge

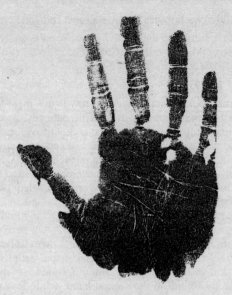

Wide Hand

Young man age twenty-four who wanted to be an astronaut. Note extra line across center of palm and unusual spacing between fingers. Technical hand but creativity is stifled.

People with action hands and technical hands should always be involved with a job that is busy, involves a variety of activities, is not a confined desk job, and offers some amount of work or activity outdoors. Sunshine and fresh air are almost a life-and-death necessity for the wide-handed, who may be a bit claustrophobic and hate to be shut up.

Some amount of travel is good for people with the action or technical type of hand, as long as the travel offers interesting scenery and some activity. Tourist traps are not for you if you belong to either group.

You are gamblers by nature and not afraid of risk, for with your clear perception, you have already found an edge.

Whatever your career, it is certain that you will have at least

one and possibly two hobbies that are almost full-time careers
in themselves.

Enjoy.

NARROW HANDS

More delicate-looking and longer, narrow hands include the
mental as well as the emotional type. This delicacy, however
may be deceptive, for some fearless competitors, such as
Barbra Streisand, have narrow hands. Her fingers are extremely flexible and uncommonly long. Her talent in a half dozen
fields is unmistakable, and she could never be considered the
"shrinking violet" that some believe narrow-handed people
are. Julia Roberts has a smaller version of the same hand.

It is fascinating to watch hands instead of faces in movies or
on television, as the hands of so many well-known personalities are very different from what you'd expect them to be.

A narrow hand has a definite rectangular shape, with fingers
as long as or longer than the palm. Smooth, round, or square-
tipped fingers are found on the mental hand, while less well-
padded, often prominently knuckled fingers belong to the
emotional type of hand.

If an imaginary line were drawn up the center of the narrow
hand, the greatest number of lines would be on the little-finger
side of the hand in most cases. The ring finger on these hands
is longer than the index.

Especially on the emotional hand, there is often a loose web
of skin between some or most of the fingers, and the web is
also sometimes apparent between the index finger and the
thumb.

Fingernails on narrow hands may be rounded and medium-
arched to high-arched, while fingertips are more often rounded than squared off, which is a trait peculiar to Sagittarians,
born in November and December.

It is more common for fingers on narrow hands to bend
inward, and this will help indicate whether the sought-for
career should be one of self-projection and public activity, or
of quiet, unobtrusive service to others. Both of these functions

are common to narrow-handed people. (Check finger bends in Chapter 10)

The skin is finer on the emotional hand than on the mental hand, and may even be loose-looking in appearance, but unless the owner is well past middle age, his or her skin wiil be tighter than it looks.

Narrow hands may look soft and ineffectual, but they possess a basic strength of emotion and character as well.

Career choices:

MENTAL HANDS

Architecture	Science
Real estate sales	Astronomer
Design	Science researcher
Stocks/Bonds/Commodities sales	Historian
Homeopath	Author
Martial arts	Actor
Psychology/Psychiatry	Music
Antiques sales or restoration	Clothing design
Art conservator	Couturier
Museum conservator	Artist
Data processor	Computer systems/theory

EMOTIONAL HANDS

Botanist	Nursing
Secretary	Romance writing
Model	Pediatrician
Word processing	Actress, actor
Receptionist	Beautician
Rehabbing and decorating houses	Cosmetician
Elder care	Sales
Pre-kindergarten teacher	Tour organizing/sales
Librarian	Musician
	Silk-screening
	Florist

Of course, there are many professions not listed here that will suit all four of these hand types.

Putting fingerprint classifications and skin patterns on both palms together with the above information should give you the beginning of good, accurate analysis of career choices and aptitude.

BLENDED HANDS

It is entirely possible that a person has a mixture of two of the four hand types. The most common blends would be the long fingers of the mental hand with the square hand of the technical type, or the rounded palm of the fire type.

If this is the case, then the already desirable traits of both hands are tempered by the cooler, patient intellect the mental hand indicates.

ACTION/MENTAL: An indication of balance, with less emphasis on the impatient reactions of the action person, and a deeper quality of mental activity. If the hand is seen to have an extremely rounded palm, and long, blunt-tipped fingers in a widespread position, it would fall into this classification. Career choices would include specialization in all of the fields covered by both action and mental types. All hands that have action as the dominant influence belong to persons who are warm and spontaneous, who read well and rapidly, and who are usually able to memorize rapidly and accurately. The addition of the mental type to an action hand may also tend to cut down on the typical fast-changing moods of the action personality. Another benefit is that action hands are rarely addictive, except to coffee first thing in the morning, and most blends with action dominance will avoid any abuse of alcohol or drugs.

ACTION/TECHNICAL: This blend is a good one, for the impulsiveness of action can be tempered by the slower thought processes of the technical mind. Such a blend is indicated by broader, longer, and bluntly rounded fingertips. These hands often look as if they might be clumsy, but they are often as graceful and sure as the hands of a magician. (Most magicians will possess hands of this blended type, as a matter of fact.) This type is a doer and an achiever with a great many projects going on at the same time, and all of them coming together nicely, thank you.

All action-dominant blends are marks of the talented and often multitalented person. Resourceful, capable, and motivated, these individuals often aspire to the highest position in any profession or company in which they find themselves, and do extremely well at having their own businesses, especially in art, food, or floral areas.

Whatever they do, the action dominance lends them a certain flair and dash that will be unlike anybody else's efforts.

To their talents add the quality of generosity. A most fortunate hand shape to have, indeed.

TECHNICAL/MENTAL: A long and squared-off hand with a rectangular palm, large and low-set thumb, and a more smoothly padded hand indicates this blend. There are more palmar lines here than on the usual technical hand. Fingers will be flexible, but either square-sided or gently rounded, possibly with a blunted tip section. This, too, is a good blend, which adds the more active mind seen in the smoothly arched fingernails. Deeply creative on its own, the basic technical personality combines with the wider aspects of creative inspiration that are the hallmarks of the mental personality. Usually voracious readers, this blended type likes to read something and then try it out. These people belong to the small group that will read an entire instruction booklet and schematic before plugging in a new appliance. Career fields are wide-ranging, adding all of the potentials of the mental hand to the technical. From rocket science to bioengineered DNA medical experimentation, this hand will be found on people in unique occupations that are on the cutting edge of technology! People with this blend have the foresight to explore untried fields and the tenacity to follow all possibilities until they reach success. There are entrepreneurs in this blended category, but just as many will find comfortable positions running their own shop within an already existing business—while pursuing imaginitive goals!

Other blends can be found in my previous book: however, you can interpret them to some extent yourself. For example, if you find that your hand seems to be the action type but you have long, knobby fingers and tons of lines all over your palm, simply add the attributes and career directions of your action-dominant hand to those of the emotional type. There will be many career directions in common from which you can choose a favorite.

5

THE FINGER OF FATE

Fingers can be fascinating, from the long, tapering digits of
Barbra Streisand, to the short-fingered round hands of Danny
DeVito.

Most of us talk with our hands, making gestures even when
on the telephone, as if our listeners can also see us. Amazingly,
this use of hands as conveyors of meaning and expression is a
habit of all cultures across the world. Gestures may differ—a
pointed finger in one country may be a rude sign, while it is a
source of some important information in another culture—but
communication with hands is universal.

Everything the hands do is important and can add much to
our understanding and acceptance of others. It is interesting to
watch the hands of public figures, religious leaders, and politi-
cians to see whether they are openhandedly telling us the truth,
or whether they curl their fingers and conceal the meaning
behind what they say. The open-palm gesture has been a sign
of nonthreatening, peacemaking sincerity in all centuries. One
of the messages this conveys is the lack of a concealed
weapon, which may be where it began.

Interestingly, people who habitually carry their hands in a

Vocations

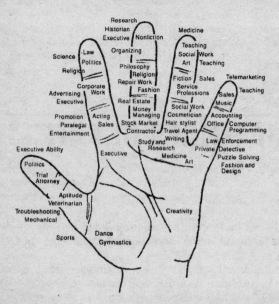

closed position or a fist are often persons who are not being truthful with themselves, not to mention those around them.

If you cannot see a person's hands, be hesitant about trusting him or her.

Hospital nursing personnel will verify that when a man or woman nears death, the thumb turns into the hand, and nurses will often be forced to put a roll of gauze in the space between forefinger and thumb to keep the thumb from curling in too far. This observation has also been made about premature newborns, or babies who are born with some health problem. In the adult, normal human, the thumb should never be carried inward as if it were another finger. This is the sign of a personality disturbance.

Some persons wake in the morning to find that their thumbs are stiff from being held in this way, or perhaps they clenched the whole hand in a fist all night. Sleep researchers have noted this as a corollary of disturbances during sleep, of personal tension and distress, and of nightmares.

In times of great upheaval, you may find you are holding your hands in a fist. A conscious decision should be made to stop this habit. You may relax the hand consciously, even flap and shake the hands hard to loosen them up. Some cultures provide fancy metal balls with bells in them to roll around in the hand and obviate this tendency; others use a short string of amber beads, or even a smooth, polished fingerstone.

I have never noted any unnatural limp-wristedness among persons who are born homosexual, but I have noted such a tendency among people with very low personal self-esteem, or some forms of glandular disease. Sufferers from Lou Gehrig's disease often exhibit this limp-wristed syndrome very early in the disease without realizing it may presage a severe health problem not yet diagnosed.

There are a great many things that can be ascertained about an individual from watching the hands, including some clear vocational or career indications.

LONG FINGERS

Long, thin or long, strong fingers may be found on two types we have already discussed—mental and emotional hands—but longer fingers can also be found on the other types, though not as commonly.

If your index finger is longer than your palm by so much as a half inch, then it would be considered long-normal. If it measures more than three-quarters of an inch to an inch longer than the palm section, it would be considered long.

Long fingers indicate that the owner's mind is clear, often uncomplicated, and unlikely to act upon pure impulse.

If your fingers are an inch or more longer than your palm, no matter what sort of palm you have, the chances are good that you will find happiness in a career where a great deal of research and memory work is required. Your thought process-

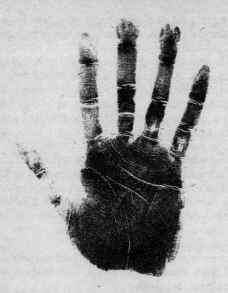

The fingers of this hand are longer than the palm. Another rarity is the longer second-finger phalanges. This woman is employed as a medical secretary in a large hospital. She is single and a writer of poetry and romantic short stories.

es are lucid, and you may like to consider more than one option before you make decisions. You may actually enjoy a career in which an invention or new ideas begin to come together and take form in reality.

Possible choices: Architecture; home building; property development; money management; producer for stage, radio, TV; scriptwriting; creating film projects or cinematography; and environmentalist/naturalist.

The longer the fingers, the more time you will require to make decisions. Overlong fingers sometimes make the owners seem hesitant about acting, just because they prefer to think things through before making any moves. This factor would also be a fine one for school administrators, city planning commission members, aldermen, church officers, and in almost any profession where long-term projects or benefits are outlined and put into practice.

Short-fingered people sometimes become angry with those who have longer fingers and accuse them of being indecisive, because they are not *moving*. At the same time, the longer-fingered can become irritated with the spontaneity of those whose fingers are short and who process and act rapidly. Both of these types are necessary in any organization, however, to provide balance. In one institution, though, this contrast can become a problem until both parties realize exactly what the problem is—and that institution is marriage. In a business partnership, these factors can be taken into consideration and used as an effective tool to create harmony. In the career of marriage, this subtle but important difference may make any mountain into a molehill—or any molehill into a mountain!

If you find that your fingers are quite short, and your partner's are longer than the palm by far, this problem should be discussed and future plans should be delegated to the one most capable of either the planning or the execution of the project. Each has his or her own best use, and should be put in a position where he or she can exercise it.

KEY WORDS: THOUGHTFUL, CONSIDERATION

SHORT FINGERS

Index fingers that are the same length as the palm would be considered a bit short on mental, emotional, and even some technical hands. If they are as much as a half inch shorter than the palm, they would be considered quite short.

Short fingers make you impulsive, sometimes hasty, and prone to ill-considered decisions or actions.

The good side is that you are the doers among us, and will usually gladly take on jobs your long-fingered brethren would never touch.

If the fingers are very short, it may be useful to look at the size of the three finger segments or phalanges. In some unusu-

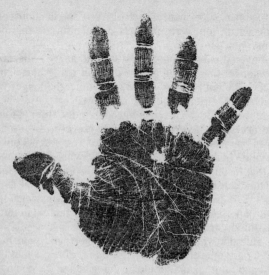

This unusual hand has very short fingers that exhibit the short tip section as well. The hand is a blend of the emotional (many lines) on a technical hand. This forty-three-year old man is a creative craftsman whose job is in restoring fine antique furniture and metal work.

al hands, all the tip sections are very much the shortest of the phalanges, and on other hands it may be the bottom portions. Often the imbalance of size will be shown on different portions of the fingers.

If the tip sections are the shortest, you are such a realist that you may have become cynical or skeptical about almost everything. This might signify a lack of imagination as well, or an inability to empathize with others.

If the bottom sections are shortest, you are usually a loner, or satisfied to make your home where your hat may be. Also you need a good measure of time alone, just to think or to relax and vegetate. Your idea of the perfect vacation would not be a cruise to the Windward Islands, but a gorgeous landscape with nobody in it but yourself!

If the shortness is not confined to the same section of all four fingers, but is divided among them, with one short section appearing somewhere on each finger, then you will use the indications in the next chapter to discover what each phalange covers and what it can mean to your life and your career.

In general, though, if your hand is of the action type, and fingers normal for that hand, or if your hand is one of the other three types and the fingers are the same length as the palm or shorter, you will be apt to do things in a hasty, sometimes impulsive way. You will be warmhearted and have the best of intentions, but will often be found with a foot hanging out of your mouth because you spoke before you thought.

Your redeeming features however, are, your readiness to perceive and to act, your caring and willingness to give assistance, and your general attitude of "let's get it done."

KEY WORDS: SPONTANEOUS, ACUTELY PERCEPTIVE

Career choices:

All Tips Short:

Engineering	Police dispatcher
Mechanics	Fireman
Construction trades	Sanitary engineer
Electrician	Videotape reproducing
Janitorial or custodial services	Assembly work
Offset lithographer	Landscaping, gardening
Small appliance repair	

All Lower Sections Short:

Acting, performing comedy routines	Writer, especially investigative journalism
Sports coach or referee	Politics
Sales representative	Musician
Real estate sales	Social work

It would be extremely rare if all of the middle sections of anyone's fingers were the shortest. Indications would be that if

Comparative Links

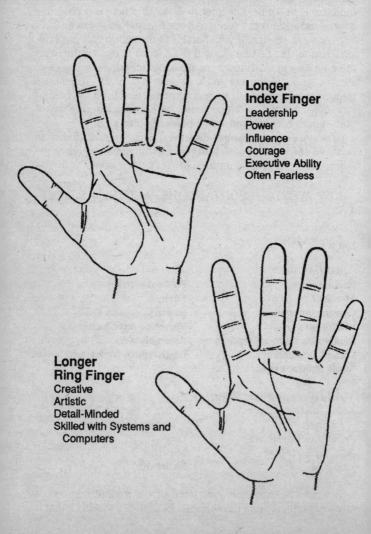

**Longer
Index Finger**
Leadership
Power
Influence
Courage
Executive Ability
Often Fearless

**Longer
Ring Finger**
Creative
Artistic
Detail-Minded
Skilled with Systems and
  Computers

this were the case on your hand, your greatest challenges lie in understanding yourself and motivating yourself. You would prefer to stay out of the limelight completely and become perhaps the power behind the throne.

The few hands I have noted that have very short second phalanges all across the hand belonged to people who were not career-oriented at all and were merely working to pay the bills while looking forward with anticipation to retiring and spending their time pursuing their own hobbies and interests.

DOMINANT FINGERS

On some hands, there is a nice balance among all of the fingers. These hands belong to adaptable and mostly well-balanced individuals. Salt of the earth, these hands are in the majority. Careerwise, a person with such hands would have to look at factors other than finger length to find the most suitable field.

There are other hands, however, that show a clear dominance in one finger or another. This may be seen in the length of either the index finger or the ring finger. Alternatively, the handprint may show a dominance not visible to the eye—one of the fingers may print much wider or much darker than any other finger on the hand.

If one of your fingers shows this dominance, it is important to understand what this adds to your personality and to your career potentials.

LONGER INDEX FINGER—THE EXECUTIVE

If the index finger when held close to the others is much longer than the ring finger, it holds a dominance. Sometimes this extra length is shown only when the hand is printed, but usually it is visible to the naked eye.

If the index finger is visibly longer to the eye or on the print, it is considered the *power* finger. It is the mark of the one who can take control of a situation, a group, or a goal. The executive finger gives you leadership, influence, courage, power,

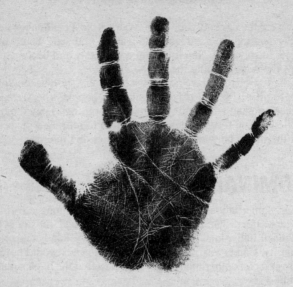

Note the dominance of this child's index finger. Its width and the darkness of the ink indicate a leader. Note the humor loop and the memory loop. The owner of this action hand will reach the top in any field she attempts, probable career direction: Gourmet cook or a professional chef.

executive ability, and often fearlessness in taking a risk. This fearless quality does not mean you choose to scale steep cliffs barehanded, or jump without a parachute from high buildings. It does mean that you are willing to step out from the crowd and take a position or set yourself apart from the masses of humanity in some positive way.

Careers: corporate executive, social engineer, entrepreneur, business owner, office manager, director or producer, law enforcement, or FBI.

Whatever position you may take as a beginning, you will realize that it *is* just a beginning and a means to an end. You will do well in any position of leadership and authority.

The sections of the finger are related respectively to the force of ambition that drives you to succeed, the ability you possess to express your inner personality, and the eternal urge to know and to learn.

This finger's length, then, adds motivation to any hand, no matter to which of the four major types or several blends it belongs.

Ambition is a prevalent quality of people with this finger dominant. Not afraid of work, those with the long index finger will work overtime and weekends if that is what it takes to get the job done and done well. This is the extra effort that allows them to reach the top in any field, and it is the one factor that all bosses and superiors notice before any other.

To know and to learn, one must put forth effort, and the long index finger gives you the desire to learn not only by your own methods, but also from listening to others who are experts in their own fields.

You will question others and you will question yourself, always reaching for that mark of excellence that you crave more than any other goal.

Although the approval of others is of utmost importance to those with the long index finger, their own self-esteem and approval are perhaps even more important.

Honesty is a factor these people appreciate in others, and most of all they learn to despise liars.

Your weakness if you have a dominant index finger is that you absolutely cannot stand to be accused of having done something you haven't done. This is definitely a trigger point, and in an employment situation you must control your temper if you are innocent and someone accuses you.

You will be filled with confidence and pride in your accomplishment, even if only you know how hard it was to maintain that tight control on your emotions.

You will do well in any position where you are in charge of other people, and you usually make a considerate and caring boss, even though you will always get the best out of your people. This dominant finger can be a ticket to success.

KEY WORDS: AMBITION, COMPETENCE

LONGER RING FINGER

Very early in the space program, I noticed that there was a definite difference among the hands of those first astronauts. The command pilots always had the long index finger, while the backup pilots, who didn't land on the moon, had the longer ring finger, the mark of the creative craftsman.

Although all of these men were licensed pilots and extremely well trained in scientific methods, those with the longer index finger always got the extremely risky missions. This was of great interest to me as I had already done much work in analyzing the significance of dominant fingers.

Long fingers, as I have said, are a departure from the so-called norm in that they almost predispose the owner to certain fields and types of activity. Naturally there were no such jobs as astronaut until after the middle 1960s, but the dominant index finger was easily found on the hands of leaders in business, finance, politics, and adventure.

The longer ring finger, however, is usually the mark of the specialist in one field or another. Creative not only in their talents and abilities, but also in their thinking, these men and women plan the activities for others to carry out.

In studying religious art of the ages for hand types and gestures, I encountered another odd fact. The creator, God, is usually depicted as having a long index finger, while the Virgin Mary is shown with an extremely long ring finger. Curiosity leads me to wish I could ask the artists why they chose this symbolism.

The ring finger is the finger of love and romance, as illustrated by our most ancient traditions, and theory had it that there was a direct connection between this finger and the heart. For this reason, it was used as the site for rings of betrothal and then of marriage.

The three sections that compose it reveal how we interact with others, our ideals and dreams, our wish to help and guide, or to be of use socially.

It represents the persona, the personality we construct to show the world. We will discuss this and its indications in a later chapter, but if this is the longest of the two power fingers on your own hand, you are probably creative in your thinking, if not with your hands. You may be guided toward work that will benefit others, not just yourself. Even if you do not admit it except to yourself, you are a bit of a romantic. Women with this long finger often get teary-eyed in sad movies, and their male counterparts do, too, whether they admit it or not.

Careers:

Artist	Nurse
Troubleshooter	Medical field
Social worker	Doctor
Teacher, professor	Nutritionist
Philosopher	Fashion
Group leader	Design
Scientist	Photographer
Computer programmer	

Although, if your ring finger is dominant, you may find it difficult to endure a job that does not suit your basic needs and talents, you will be able to motivate yourself to do it and do it well, just so long as you are working toward the necessary education or training you will require to change your field to something that would be much more to your liking.

If you have a fault, it is that you are willing to go that extra mile too many times. You take such pride in your work that you will often let others take advantage of your willingness. The old saying is "too good for your own good," and that is something you should remember. No job is worth letting someone take unnecessary advantage of your goodwill. This can lead to physical exhaustion and eventually to illness.

Outgoing, caring, and considerate, you fill your life with friends, interests, and projects.

KEY WORDS: CREATIVE, GIVING

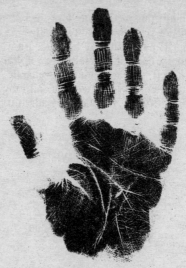

An emotional hand with a low-set little-finger. The owner is shy, sensitive, and loving. Her profession as computer details organizer is offset by her very creative skill at dressmaking, crafts, and floral arranging. She is also a seashell collector.

LONG LITTLE FINGER

This finger indicates your ability to communicate, your ability to assess your inner or true self, your ability to solve problems, as well as your sexual (sensuality) index.

If this finger is very long, it is best to measure each phalange separately, to see if there is a dominance and in which area it lies.

It is possible to have a dominant little finger from base to tip, and if you do, it marks you as an expert at some form of communication and puzzle-solving, someone who is able to accept him or herself as is.

Careerwise, it could indicate a specialist in some form of media, writing, or advertising, or a writer of detective stories, depending on the balance of the finger sections.

LOW-SET LITTLE FINGER

If the little finger is very low set on the hand, the person tends to be somewhat diffident and shy. There is little wish to push into the limelight or to call attention to oneself. Career indications: Any career that does not call for leadership; any career that allows the individual flexibility; any career that offers puzzles to be solved; and anything involving invention or innovation.

This shyness is sometimes overcome in childhood, and the individual will learn to communicate easily and to interact in public without distress.

The attempt to overcome this is sometimes so successful that the individual will enter a career as a comedian, but his or her comedy will be mostly about personal faults and foibles, in the Rodney Dangerfield "I don't get no respect" vein.

This is also the most commonly observed aspect on the hands of actors and other performers who suffer from intense stage fright.

KEY WORD: HESITANT, SHY, OVERLY SELF-AWARE

HIGH-SET LITTLE FINGER

The reverse of the low-set little finger, this indication belongs to a person who may be too ready to communicate.

Even without a whorl or bull's-eye fingerprint, if this fingertip is the longest on the finger, then it can truly earn the term "telephone finger," because it is usually dialing someone else's number!

This higher-set position also pushes the person into some aspects of public self-examination. If he or she feels guilty about something, it will be no secret to friends and family. If all criminals had this high setting of the little finger, the police would have easier jobs, for the wrongdoers would all confess their misdeeds to all and sundry.

If you have this high-set finger, you must be careful not to become overbearing, to talk others to death, or to be pushy in your relationships with them.

High set little finger. Each fingerprint is different: a double-looped middle
finger, a radial loop on the index finger, a whorl on the ring finger, and a
peacock feather on the little finger. This technical hand belongs to a
research psychologist whose hobby is playing music.

You may well have a positive genius for some kind of communication, and you should seek to discover what this may be.
A more complete analysis of the hand may reveal it, and this
can be backed up by some type of professional aptitude testing.
When you discover what it is, get back into some training program to develop this ability.

Careers:

Anything that involves use of
  the voice
Careers in media
News anchor
Investigative journalism
Talk show host

Teaching voice or singing
Private detective or lawyer's
  investigator
Home shopping channel host
Motivational seminar leader
Minister, evangelist,
  preacher

The most important thing to remember if you have this high finger placement is to guard your tongue and count to ten before you speak in haste or in anger.

KEY WORD: VERBOSITY, EAGERNESS

THE THUMB

This finger should be balanced in its segments and neither too highly set nor too low on the hand. The portions of the thumb represent the attributes of willpower and determination, logical and intuitive thinking. The base, which is actually within the palm, denotes the basic strength of your personality.

A HIGH-SET THUMB

If the thumb is so high set that it looks like one of the other fingers, or is held high and close to the index finger, it is an indication of the kind of personality that tends to hold things in and be secretive.

This can be a temporary thing, as any of you who set out to get handprints of your family and friends will instantly notice, for many people will agree to let you take their print, but will then hold all the fingers tightly together in a stiff "flipper" as if they were going to go swimming. For this reason, it is best to take the subject's hand and literally shake it when it is inked, and then bring it down onto the paper quickly before it can stiffen up again.

If the thumb is still sticking to the side of the index finger after you have made the print, then just quietly watch the person until he or she has washed the hand, and you will see if this is a true indication, if the thumb is always held close to the index.

Should this be the case, then the person is still hiding something from you, or from the world. Often people who feel that they want their hands analyzed for career information or other reasons will assume that all of their secrets will be revealed. You must reassure them that you are not going to know when

This thirty-two year old woman has both a high-set thumb and a narrow hand. She has a strong lower thumb phalange, which helps to balance the high thumb. She has had problems with a gambling addiction and feels that she should be an artist rather than a librarian. Her creativity is stifled. Note horizontal lines beneath ring finger.

they will die, or if they are going to be revealed as an income-tax evader, or anything else.

It is a fact that 100 percent of the criminal handprints I have in my files are "flippers," with thumb and fingers held tightly together. Apparently, when being printed, these people were still hoping that they could keep some of their activities secret.

A high-set thumb that is *not* held close to the other fingers is the mark of a person who may not be in touch with his or her own feelings. Intuition may war with logic in this person, and the tip section of the thumb may be crossed with deep horizontal lines indicating frustration.

If your thumb is set too high, you may have had a problem all of your life in making decisions because of this internal war between logic and intuition. You may have found that no matter what decision you made, a small voice inside kept nagging you that you may have made a mistake. The result could be progress impeded by indecision.

If this is the case, and the lines of frustration do show on the thumb, then you should do a complete analysis of the rest of the hand to see if something else will offset this inability to see your way clearly. Sometimes the third phalange of the thumb, which is inside the palm itself, will be of good size and firmly padded. This could add strength to the entire hand.

If this third section *is* firmly padded and of good size, and there is some indication on the rest of the hand that you might be talented and competent in certain particular careers, then you may find that some of your indecision can be averted by moving into one of those fields and taking any extra training available to enhance that ability and advance your future earning potential.

Should you find that you are still having trouble making decisions, then you might want to seek counseling for personal problems, and to help you sort out your business affairs.

High-set thumbs often mark the person who encounters some financial problems through overuse of credit cards. If this is a problem for you, seek out free financial counseling in your community. Most banks and libraries will have the number to call on file.

The high-set thumb is also the mark of a person who will marry in haste and repent at leisure, as the saying goes. A good comparison analysis of both hands might help avert this problem. If it has already occurred, consult a family counseling service for help and advice.

KEY WORD: UNCERTAINTY

LOW-SET THUMB

A low-set thumb can be an indication of a positive talent for one or another kind of sports activity, or it can indicate that you are a person who is prone to trust everyone you meet.

The sports thumb is unmistakable. Look carefully at the

This fifty-five year old male hand is that of a professional baseball player who is now an electronics engineer. Note the offset sports thumb, and the electronics skin pattern above the heart line. The second and third sections of the little finger are not visible due to severe gastric disturbance.

illustration above and you will see that the sports thumb is set onto the hand at an angle—almost as if there were a fourth phalange on this thumb.

I first confirmed this when a student in one of my public school classes brought in the prints of her family for comparison. It had been in my mind for some time, but when she put down a huge print with the unusual offset thumb showing clearly, I took a chance and asked, "Does your brother do something in sports?" She laughed and said, "He's with the Green Bay Packers"!

From that time on, whenever I saw this thumb, whether on a male or female hand, I found that it denoted a person whose interest or actual participation in sports was one of his or her most outstanding characteristics.

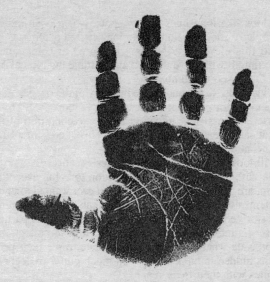

This child's hand has a very low-set, drooping thumb. This thumb should be offset as it is a sports thumb. Upon the child's recovery from serious illness, the thumb will return to its natural position.

The physical body is usually in good shape, and if you have this offset "sports" thumb, you will probably enjoy exercise, even as a part-time activity.

Although the low-set thumb is not always an offset thumb, this subdivisional group is an important portion of the general category.

Only illness or disability can change the aspect of the offset thumb, as you will note in the print of the small child that shows a thumb drooping downward at almost a right angle. This hand is that of a child who was born with a serious birth defect and, because of constant and physically traumatic health problems and surgery, has not been able to develop the activity and talent he should possess in some area of sports.

The skin patterns all over the hand and fingers are broken

up, and look like long lines of tiny spots, which is an indication of toxicity and infection over a long period of illness.

Should this eleven-year-old boy be cured at some future time, the thumb will move upward and assume the typical off-set look of the sports thumb.

The illness also accounts for the inability of the outside edge of the hand to print fully. It has a striking "scooped-off" look. The cause is a persistent infection and toxic condition of the blood that can spread to the entire body. This hand is much too small for that of an eleven-year-old.

We will look forward to this youngster's recovery.

People with low-set thumbs, in addition to being accepting and warm, are prone to telling you all you ever wanted to know about themselves. Engaging, cheerful, and often charming, they are storytellers, raconteurs, and a definite asset at parties!

Low-set thumbs also mark people who love to collect, and they appreciate what they collect. They hate to see their prize specimens hidden in bank vaults, and much prefer to decorate their homes with their treasures.

Someone with this sort of hand also loves growing plants and flowers, and if there is such a thing as a "green thumb," it will be a deeply set one. If you have a low-set thumb, you will undoubtedly prefer a basket of flowers to a box of candy, and will enjoy just looking at gardening magazines and seed catalogs.

Low-set thumb career choices:

Convention organizing	Fountain pen collector
Tour planner	Nonfiction writer
Antiques appraiser	Journalist
Flea market owner	Poet
Gemologist	Musician

High-set thumb careers:

Travel agent	Computer operator
Secretary	Dressmaker
Office worker	Cosmetician

Sports thumb career choices:

Football or baseball coach	Sporting equipment
Team manager	salesperson
Referee	Gymnasium operator
Sports columnist	Aerobics instructor
Sports reporter for TV or radio	Martial arts instructor

If there is a finger on the hand that exhibits a wider size and prints in a much darker shade than the others, it should be considered a dominant finger.

The next chapter will cover these dominances more specifically as they relate to vocation or career, and how they should be analyzed.

KEY WORD: PHYSICAL/ACTIVITY

6

YOUR FINGERS ARE
YOUR FORTUNE

All of your fingers have not only length and width, but also three distinctly separate sections.

On most hands, these sections are divided by deep-cut lines that are referred to as flexure lines, because doctors once thought they were caused by bending the fingers. As a matter of fact, doctors once called all of the hand's lines flexure creases, as it was thought that all of them could be explained by how the hand bent when it was used.

Today, however, with the added knowledge that these lines and creases are present on the hands of even a newborn, and that in the years after birth their number may remain the same or may double in amount, this notion has been dismissed. No one had ever successfully explained how a hand could have deep lines and creases in places where it cannot physically bend at all!

No hand has ever had a complete balance among the sizes of all finger sections. Each finger will have size differences among its three segments or phalanges. It is precisely this dif-

106

The Finger Rulerships

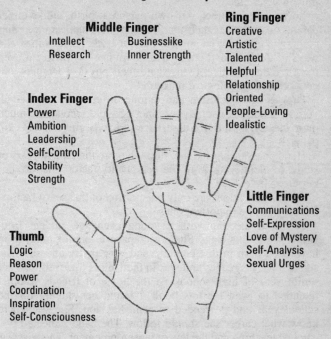

Middle Finger
Intellect   Businesslike
Research   Inner Strength

Ring Finger
Creative
Artistic
Talented
Helpful
Relationship
Oriented
People-Loving
Idealistic

Index Finger
Power
Ambition
Leadership
Self-Control
Stability
Strength

Little Finger
Communications
Self-Expression
Love of Mystery
Self-Analysis
Sexual Urges

Thumb
Logic
Reason
Power
Coordination
Inspiration
Self-Consciousness

ference in size and dominance that makes you an individual, and along with the skin patternings themselves, makes you different from any other person walking the earth, today, yesterday, or tomorrow.

You do not inherit these differences from your parents. A very slight similarity will exist among siblings and parents. As we know, our hands reflect the patternings of the DNA, and when we are conceived we receive in varying patterns chromosomes from both ancestral lines. This is why DNA testing can tell you that your own patterns are shared by only two or three individuals in all the millions that are alive at this time, and even this similarity may concern only a tiny portion of the immense genome.

So we are, in effect, our own person at birth, unlike either parent or any one ancestor. Our physical appearance, hair color, and eyes can be similar, but our basic personalities and ways of thinking and doing will be immensely different even from a twin. Identical twins share their physical features, but never their psychological makeup.

How is this exclusive and unique difference expressed in your own body? First by your inner eye, and second and much more clearly, by the size and shape of hands, fingers, and skin patterns.

Hand analysis has led me, through more than thirty years of study, to identify some of the personality factors that are our keys to self.

Career indications are only one portion of that set of factors, but they can be important ones.

A recent meeting with a young exchange student from Brazil made this clear. She was Japanese, one of many who have been born in that country, and very pretty and shy. She spoke three languages and was in the United States to take her senior year of high school. At the home of friends whom I intended to print for this book, I found her staying for the school year and proceeded to print her, too. She wanted to know what career she should follow. The hand indicated two careers: teaching and the law or law enforcement. This girl was amazed, for she had been vacillating between pursuing a college education in the teaching of English, or a prelaw course leading to a career as an attorney.

Judging from her evident shyness and her low-set little finger, Marcia would be better suited in a teaching career than in the hurly-burly of law. Both ring finger and little finger tips were elongated, and there were several other indications of the good and sincere teacher. I have asked her to let me know which career she chooses in the years to come.

Teaching, of course, is a broad term, stretching from preschool or headstart classes into the realm of the college professor. There are other ways of teaching—through example,

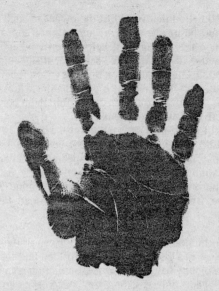

Exchange student, age 15, Long tip on INDEX, Large tip on Ring finger, action hand high-set thumb.

through books, videocassettes, and audio-visual or CD-ROM mechanisms. Plus, there is the field of posteducational teaching of adults in hobbies, crafts, sports, and mind-enriching subjects. The hand of a person who has the ability and capacity to outline a subject to others in any of these ways, so that someone else is able to understand new information, is teaching, and it is not a universal talent. There are thousands upon thousands of individuals who are knowledgeable in a specific subject or who possess a specific talent, art, or skill for creating something, and yet are not able to impart an understanding of the subject to anyone else.

The long tip on the ring finger indicates one who is concerned with the benefit or welfare of others, driven by a desire to help humanity. With the long tip on the little finger, indicating one who can communicate thoughts and methods, you have a combination that would fit the owner of such a hand to teach. Should he or she never acquire a skill appropriate for teaching, then this person will help in some other way. This finger formation also marks the social scientist, social worker, doctor, specialist nurse, and soon in some cases, this finger formation is seen on the hands of a good parent who is given to teaching his or her own children and urging them constantly to acquire more education for themselves.

If the girl I mentioned does not choose a career in teaching, she should become an attorney not for corporate legal work, not for prosecution, but for some specialized area of legal defense. Examination of other markings on the palmar area might be more instructive in helping to determine which she will choose. These indications will be outlined in the next chapter.

Finger formations can be so specific. Even in the newborn, although there is a general look of unformed and fat little fingers upon a blobby hand, if careful examination is made, a distinct hand shape emerges, and tiny differences in size and length are seen in one or more fingers.

Skin patterns are already formed completely, of course, and it was from this factor that several researchers, including Dr. Milton Alter of the Minneapolis V.A. Hospital, discovered that congenital heart defects in the newborn can be determined from handprint analysis.* Other medical researchers confirmed this finding and were hard at work in determining other such skin pattern or skin line anomalies that gave clues to genetic birth defects and DNA abnormalities.

In addition to this valuable research, it has been the work of myself and my colleagues to determine vocational factors in skin pattern or size differential that are as valid as those early medical findings.

Part of this research involves the discovery that on the hands of criminals or persons inclined to violence, the incidence of a specific double-looped or whorled print on the thumb may be a genetic marker. In classwork I've found that it's possible to

* "Hearts and Palms," Medicine, *Newsweek*, Sept. 14, 1970

obscure the photo and "wanted" details on an FBI flier and have the students correctly identify the type of crime for which the individual was sought!

Unfortunately, in most cases only the fingerprints of the criminal are taken, so that the information that could be gained from the palmar prints and sizes is lost.

HOW TO MEASURE FINGER SECTIONS

Finger sections, or phalanges, are measured with a six-inch ruler held at the base of the finger.

It is not always easy to measure the finger by holding the ruler between fingers, because some hands have a skin flap called a "web" between fingers. This is true especially of the emotional hand. The web indicates a person whose emotions rule their personality, while a wide, taut area between fingers indicates the ability to use the mind to control the emotions.

It is best to measure the fingers by placing the ruler on the palm itself, exactly where the flexure lines *begin*. After this phalange is measured, then you may use the ruler at the side of the finger exactly where the knuckle bends. An accurate measurement cannot be gained from the back of the hand. It is also feasible to measure from a handprint, but not as accurate, since flexure lines may actually wander far upward or downward into a finger's inner surface, and not indicate where the knuckle bends at all.

Most hands will have phalanges of $3/4$ to $1^1/2$ inches unless the fingers are extremely long. On some male hands the phalanges may be $1^5/8$ inches or even longer if they are the dominant ones on the fingers.

Dominance is reflected in the length of the finger, the darkness of its print when the entire hand is printed, or sometimes in a widening of the phalange itself.

FAT-FINGERED COOKS AND REALISTS

One of the first interesting observations I made when my study of the hand began more than thirty years ago was that some persons have a wider section on the base of the index finger than others. Adroit questioning revealed that the widened phalange belonged most often to people who absolutely *loved* to cook. They may have hated housework drudgery, but hand them a pan and a spatula, and they were in their glory.

In fact, the two things seemed to go together—if the love for cooking existed, the distaste for cleaning dust and dirt was present, too. These individuals also seemed to be the kind of cooks who measure by a "pinch" rather than a teaspoon. Natural experts at taste, they use random combinations of flavors to

The hand of a child of one year. Note the offset (sports) thumb and the long tip on the ring finger. The index finger is dominant at this point and may continue to be as the child grows.

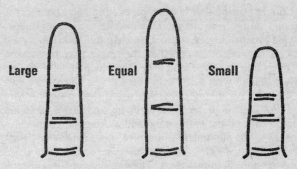

Finger sections Vary in Relation to Size

create a culinary symphony. They might look at a written recipe—in fact, many of them collected plain or exotic cook-books—but once having glanced over it, they disregard it and use their own combinations.

Recognizing this, I looked at my own hand and found that I, too, was a fat-fingered cook, a blood-bound member of that fraternity apparently dedicated never to use a measuring cup.

Of course, this widening is not reserved exclusively for good or gourmet cooks. Any of the fourteen finger sections can be wide. Each represents an accentuation of the meaning of that phalange. Note the hand of the one-year-old boy on the previous page. He has the mark of the cook already. Oddly, most of the world's great chefs are men. And he may well grow up to join their ranks. If not, he will push his wife aside and insist on cooking some or all of the meals. He should be advised not to marry a woman with the same finger, right?

A certain "tightening" of a phalange can occur, too. In the reverse of the above, this tightening acts as a constriction rather than an accentuation. Often a person who has suffered some kind of crisis, trauma, or deep psychological hurt shows it by either a deep scar or this tightening of the phalange.

If this person is accidentally employed in the field this finger section represents, he or she will dislike or even hate the work and will long for the day that it can be given up.

One finger section that is often pinched in baby boomers is the second on the ring finger. This middle section represents ideals and dreams, hopes, wishes, and aspirations. If these are injured, as they so often are, then the finger may be marked with a deep line or gouge, and it may be pinched, as if it were actually pulled in with a tiny belt. You will see this more clearly if, while taking a handprint, you use a lead pencil or thin marker and hold it perfectly straight up and down, drawing completely around the entire hand and all fingers, being careful to follow the natural line and not to squeeze the pencil against the fingers' sides. You will have seen several of these outlined handprints in this book. They are useful for outlining these small dominances or constrictions of fingers and palm. An entire book could be written about the various combinations and patterns of these varying shapes and sizes.

Many psychological and dozens of health indicators will also be revealed by thus drawing the perfect outline of a hand. Not even a hologram of the hand could be so definitive. One member of our group of hand analysts invented a method of using model-making latex to make a complete mold of any hand, which would then be used to cast a replica in acrylic or plaster mixed with papier maché. This could be a fascinating project for a family with several children, but care must be used to choose a nontoxic molding material that won't heat as it cures, which might cause a burn.

This could be a fine science project for a youngster or teenaged student to try.

The fingers may be of varying lengths, and there will also be a slight difference in the sizes of one phalange as compared to the other two finger sections. This might be:

INDEX	MIDDLE	RING	LITTLE
Tip 1″	Tip 5/8″	1″	3/4″
Middle 1 1/2″	Middle 1 1/4″	Ring 1 1/2″	Middle 1″
Bottom 1″	Bottom 1 1/2″	Bottom 1″	Bottom 1 1/2″

These size differences may seem accidental, but they are not. The middle finger is normally the longest, but the three

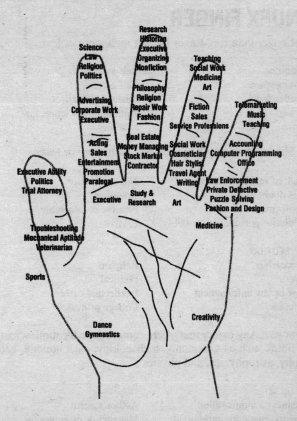

sections will have distinct variances in size, and these differences will have direct influence on your talents and vocational aptitudes.

Once you have measured all fingers, mark these measurements on the handprint or into a notebook.

The first career indications will be the relative size of the index finger as compared to the ring finger, as we saw in Chapter Five. This would give dominance to this finger as a starting point.

INDEX FINGER

Longer than ring finger by half inch more or less:

Ambition
Competence
Leadership
Power
Drive

Self-awareness
Self-esteem
Searching intellect
Aptitude for science, law,
    acting

Shorter than ring finger by half inch more or less:

Lack of self-confidence
Self-doubt
Conformity
Addictive personality (possibly)

Not an initiator
Compliant
Flexible or adaptable
Passive

TIP SECTION
Leadership
Power
Law or law enforcement
Science

Religion
Political
Intellectual career
College professor

LONGEST: Any career that offers continuous education, scientific fields such as astronomy, archaeology, paleontology, geography, astrophysics, and physics

MEDIUM:
Business administration
Any job in a corporation that
    leads to advancement
Executive secretary
Motivational promotion
Sales position
Business owner

Author's agent
Manager or promoter for
    talented individuals
Advertising agency
Corporate representative
Specialist consultant

SHORTEST: Scientific fields such as microbiology, DNA research, forensics, executive assistant, law clerk, and court reporter.

MIDDLE SECTION
LONGEST:

Advertising

Any corporate job

Real estate sales

Business owner

Interior designer

Management consultant

Department head

F.B.I.

Government position

MEDIUM:

Office manager

Sales manager

Nonfiction writer

Antiques dealer

Scientist

Computer programmer

SHORTEST: office work, salesman, craftsman, tradesman, and retail sales.

BOTTOM SECTION
LONGEST:

Acting, singing, dancing

Sales

Promotion

Paralegal

Theater management

Professional musician

Chef

Composer

Florist

MEDIUM:

Restaurant

Romance writer

Historian

Historical writer

Antiques appraiser

Police dispatcher

Technician

SHORTEST:

Hospital work

Receptionist

Secretary

Layout or pasteup art

Costume designer

Builder

Pharmacist

Cook

If this section shows dominance by a widening rather than a lengthening, then you may assign the same values as you would if it were the longest of the three.

MIDDLE FINGER

This finger is normally the longest on the hand. It should be considered as normal unless it is more than an inch longer than any other finger, or shorter than either the index or the ring finger.

TIP SECTION
LONGEST:

Organizer	Industrial management
Research	Business owner
Historical writer	Surveyor
Executive	Statistical analyst

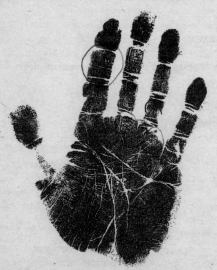

This fifty-five year old male has an extremely rare skin pattern: A loop on the base of the ring finger. He left a lucrative corporate job to become a diplomatic attaché. Note the extremely dominant index finger, with a long middle section, humor loop, and a common-sense loop give him a well-balanced personality.

YOUR CAREER IS IN YOUR HANDS

Journalism, reporter
Business consultant
Stockbroker

Librarian
Travel agency
Investor

MEDIUM
Newspaper or magazine writer
Forensic sciences
Jewelry shop owner
Chemist
College professor

Troubleshooter
Writing for stage or screen
Television production
Cinematographer
Any job involving management or organization

SHORTEST:
Inventor
Product management
Retail management or sales
Video rental store owner
Price guide author

Antiques investor
Coin expert
Import/export
Shop owner

MIDDLE SECTION
LONGEST:
Philosophy
Psychologist
Marriage counselor
Family services
Repair and restoration of antiques
Home furnishings sales
Fashion
Clock or watch repair

Jewelry design
Photography
Education
Psychiatry
Childcare
Obstetrics
Home improvement design

MEDIUM:
Floral design
Botanist
Naturalist
Earth sciences
Biologist
Chemist
Fashion sales

Cosmetics
Beautician, hairstylist
Government agencies
Forestry, park ranger
Conservationist
Veterinarian

SHORTEST:
Fast-food manager
Telephone company
Printing industry
Computer operator
Mail order sales

Clothing sales
Plant nursery work
Poet
Medical technician

BOTTOM SECTION
LONGEST:
Real Estate sales or broker
Land development
Builder
Money managing
Stock or commodity broker
Home contractor

Family planning
Farm or ranch owner
Telephone surveys
Business manager
Fiction writer

MEDIUM:
Banking industry
Computer sales
Architecture
Land surveyor

Military
D.E.A. (Drug Enforcement
   Agency)
Environmentalist
Engineer

SHORTEST:
Photographer
Handyman
Flea market operator
Electrical engineering
Meter reader

Delivery
Insurance company
Dance instructor
Landscaper

RING FINGER

This finger outlines your innate creativity. If it is long, it is
the mark of the craftsman or specialist in some creative pursuit.
Two of its sections have to do with how you interact with other
human beings. If either of these is the longest, you will spend

some or all of your time working with or for others in a help-ful way.

Longer than index by one-half inch more or less:

Good listener	Artistic talent
Motivated to service career	Psychologist
Technical skills	People-oriented
Social engineering	

Shorter than index finger by one-half inch more or less:

Unassuming	Peacemaker
Practical	Unadventurous
Realistic	Daydreaming
Judgmental	

TIP SECTION

LONGEST:

Directing	Social work
Teaching children	Medical specialties
Teaching adults	Anesthetist
Teaching disadvantaged	Art
Special education	Commercial art

MEDIUM:

Nursing	Therapeutic touch
Art	Social work
Emergency medicine	Psychologist
Pharmacist	Teaching
Music therapy	

SHORTEST:

Cartoonist	Charity work in emergency division
Fireman	
Paramedic assistant	Red cross
Hospital worker	Audiovisual technician

MIDDLE SECTION ✓

LONGEST:

Presentation sales
Real Estate
Insurance
Art or music
Teaching preschoolers
City planner

Wedding photographer
Bridal consultant
Architect
Interior decorator
Muralist
Inspirational writer

MEDIUM:

Aerobics instructor
Sports equipment sales
Shoe designer
Fabric sales
Dressmaker/tailor

Fashion industry
Model
Wedding planner
Magazine or newspaper work
Color therapist

SHORTEST:

Research technician
Medical receptionist or assistant
Inhalation therapist
Personal trainer

Ski instructor
Skater/instructor
Cosmetician
Pharmacist

BOTTOM SECTION

LONGEST:

Social worker
Diplomat
Negotiator for police
Mediator
Cosmetician

Hairstylist
Fashion consultant
Travel agent
Fiction writer

MEDIUM:

Government worker
Aerospace industry
Engineer
Tour director
Program director for cruise lines
Import/export

Fashion or apparel shop
Owning own business
Teaching
Commercial art
Computer artist

SHORTEST: Family counselor, Commercial fast-print services, creating interactive computer games, and short stories.

LITTLE FINGER

This finger indicates your capacity and your ability to both communicate and to absorb the communications of others. It should be neither too high (equal to base of ring finger) nor too low (one inch below the base of middle finger). If it is of moderate length and evenly set into the hand, the need to communicate and to listen will be strong but not extreme. If the tip section is longest, there will be a need to both give and receive communication in a strong public and even stronger intimate way. If the tip section is obviously the longest on the hand, you should be aware that you must have one friend or loved one with whom you can talk with complete freedom, to whom you can say anything at all and know that he or she would accept it without criticism.

In marriage, this is even more critical. I cannot stress too strongly the need for people with this little finger to remain single until they can find a person to whom they can talk freely. Secondly, someone with this finger must be able to be a listener and to have patience in helping his or her partner open up to share and communicate in all areas of life. We will go over some of this in more detail in the next chapter. But it is important to remember that communication needs extend to your career as well as your personal life. If your little finger indicates this need for communication, never take a job that requires you to be seen and not heard.

TIP SECTION

LONGEST:

Sales	Teaching adults enrichment
Telemarketing	courses
Teaching	Dance
Songwriting	Restaurant owner
Art photographer	Food service and caterer
	Mail order sales

MEDIUM:

Crafts/hobby instructor
Inventor
Sculpting
Writing nonfiction
Psychologist

Teaching a specialty
Hand analyst
Astrologer
Portrait artist
Fashion sketches

SHORTEST:

Office work
Computer programming
Retail sales
Musician

Education or academic-related
  field
Financial analyst
Gossip columnist

MIDDLE SECTION

LONGEST:

Certified public accountant
I.R.S. agent
Government employee
Computer programming
Entrepreneur
Musical instrument sales
School board officer

Corporate officer
Systems analyst
Chemist/chemical engineer
Optician
Anatomist
Forensics expert

MEDIUM: ✓

Accountant
Business owner
City government
Political assistant

Statistician
Poll taker
Office work

SHORTEST:

Zoology
Botany, plant culture
Rancher, farmer
Animal breeder
Cabinetmaker
Library sciences
Research assistant

Pet photographer
Gardener
Legal counselor
Behavioral research
Radiologist
Microsurgeon
Sports medicine

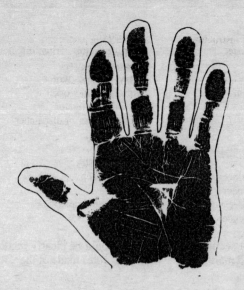

The hand of a forty-eight-year-old male police officer. His specialties are in crime reconstruction and community relations (large bottom sections on ring and little fingers), and he is also an amateur actor in local theatrical groups in his spare time (note enlarged base of dominant index finger). He is also a good to excellent cook.

BOTTOM SECTION
LONGEST:

Law enforcement
Fashion design
Biologist
Egyptology, archaeology
Paleontology
Anthropology
Field researcher
Puzzle solver or puzzle creator

Private investigator
Fiction writer
Fantasy or science fiction
 author
Police sciences
Criminal justice
Lawyer
Laser surgeon

MEDIUM:

Sports therapy
Sports broadcaster
Detective
Researcher
Photojournalism
Safari guide
Science

Forestry
Motion picture writer, director
Dinosaur expert
Travel articles writer
Rescue team worker
Arson investigator
Police officer or dispatcher

SHORTEST:
Hand analyst
Aerospace engineer
Chemical engineer
Sex therapist
Behavioral sciences

Food industry
Sports coach
Pilot
Physical therapist

    The largest section of each finger should be clearly marked with a colored marker on the print, and notes made of the voca-

Long Tip—
Lacks Reason and Logic

Short Tip—
Little Willpower

tional indications of each. A general or specific field or related study field that will emerge as the strongest career indication.

For instance, a large tip section on the ring and little fingers indicates that the subject should be teaching, but what you should teach may be determined by the largest section on one of the other two fingers. A long tip section on the index finger might indicate that the subject would be best at teaching law or constitutional issues, perhaps social studies for high school. You will need an education degree, which is usually a two-year course of study. Then you may take courses to enhance your ability and knowledge in one of these fields. A long bottom section on the index might indicate that you should be teaching drama, acting, cooking, or some area of design art. A long tip on the middle finger might indicate you should be teaching business administration, and so on.

Putting the pieces together is not difficult, once a complete analysis of all indications is completed. A lined notebook sheet can be filled out to list the applicable indications from the preceding chapters.

If two or three of the finger sections indicates a career in writing, then this person should enroll in academic or adult education courses in creative writing. His or her aptitude for fiction, reporting, news analysis, romance or historical writing, poetry, or short-story writing will soon be apparent. After someone knows the field he or she excells in, training or education in that field can be pursued.

THUMB

The thumb indicates no specific career directions in its third phalange, but the first two sections may be compared to see which is longest and to provide some direction.

TIP SECTION LONGEST:

Executive ability	Financial field
Politics	Inspirational speaker
Business ownership	Motivational instructor

MIDDLE SECTION LONGEST:

Engineering   Systems analyst
Corporate troubleshooter   Medical or biological research
Scientist   Veterinarian
Mechanical engineer

A protrusion at the base of the middle section, which usually creates the offset thumb, is an indication that your best field involves physical activities and sports of one type or another. This bump also frequently stands alone and in this case may indicate that you have a temper you must learn to control.

This forty-year-old male is a teacher. He has the teacher's square marking under his index finger. He teaches business law, which can be assumed from the long tips on the index and middle fingers. An unusual whorl on his thumb indicates willpower.

Oddly, this sometimes goes with sports ability, as in the case of tennis players like Jimmy Connors and John McEnroe, and any hockey or football team.

We will cover some psychological attitudes in the next chapter, which may help you understand how best to approach your most satisfying career, and how to do well in it.

7

STRUCTURING GOALS

The dominance of one finger section on each digit is as instructive about you and how you approach all areas of life as it is about vocational aptitudes.

Often a person struggles all his or her life in a low-echelon job, not understanding why he or she has never reached the higher position this person feels he or she deserves. Many times this is because the person's attitudes and behavior are less desirable than he or she thinks; or the person's ability to interact with coworkers might be less than satisfactory. As well, it is usually quite apparent to bosses and supervisors that some workers just seem to have no goals or aspirations, and these people, unwilling to go the extra mile, are overlooked when promotion time comes.

This personality profile can be easily seen on the hand, and can be instructive to you not only as a potential employee in a new field, but also if you are already in a position to supervise others, where it will assist you to assess their potential and quality.

Some of this is indicated by the skin lines on various sectors of the hand, especially the major lines and those on the pads under the fingers, around the edges of the palm itself.

There are also lines of activity that are cut vertically into the finger sections, beginning at the base and running upward toward the fingertip.

IDEA LINES

These lines were usually referred to as "idea lines" when I began real analysis of the hand, and indeed they still represent activity and thought in the areas where they are seen. But more, where they are thickest they accentuate the vocational areas.

Basic key words for each finger:

Thumb:	I will
Index:	I am
Middle:	I study
Ring:	I teach
Little:	I communicate

These key words apply to the length and dominance of the fingers as well as the number of lines appearing on their sections.

If few lines are clustered only on the bottom sections of your hand then you are like an unborn child, not knowing in which direction you should go. A very young child may actually lack any of these activity and thought lines, but it is not common on the adult hand.

Usually there will be a greater number of such lines on the base or bottom sections, fewer on the middle sections, and even fewer on the tips. This is natural, as we frequently have a lot more good ideas than we put into practice!

If there is a dominant finger on the handprint, wider, darker, or longer than the average, it is important to check carefully for

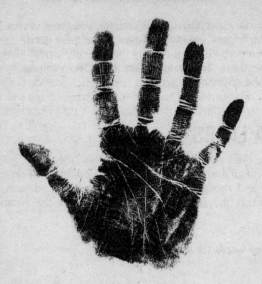

This is the hand of famed historical romance author Charlene Cross. The hand shows a triple writer's fork on the head line, a strong career line, a creative line under the ring finger, plus a very strong dream line coming upward from the outside lower edge of the hand. Note that the career line branches off in a sharp angle toward the index finger.

the number of these lines on it, as well as how high on the finger they may reach.

Look carefully at the hand of famed romance writer Charlene Cross in this chapter. Having seen her hand over a period of ten years, I have watched with interest as the struggling young unpublished author completed manuscript after manuscript only to have them returned for some trivial reason. Part of the reason was that she had been writing for the contemporary "modern-day heroines" market. At that time, she had deep blocks on all three phalanges of the little finger and was somewhat frustrated by unsuccessful writing. There were no vertical lines on the tip section, and only a few on the ring fingertip.

Today, however, with seven extremely successful romances under her belt, written from the historical perspective she has overcome the blocks represented by those horizontal lines, and the vertical lines have reached the tips of both fingers.

I have seen almost exactly the same indications on the hands of many other writers. Their hands may exhibit large and well-formed writer's forks on the middle transverse or head line, but success is a matter of effort and hard work as well as native ability. You do not climb the ladder of reward without this work. Note the large number of idea lines on the lower sections of the ring and little fingers. Charlene has a great many more stories to tell.

If you are just beginning in a career, or have not been happy with the vocation you felt was best for you, it could be that

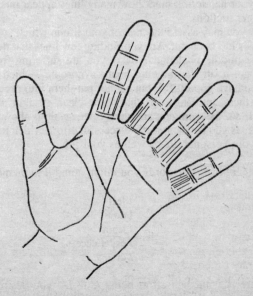

Activity or thought lines begin on the bottom finger sections and rise vertically toward the tips. Lines on the tips represent accomplishment or achievement.

you, like Charlene, are merely mistaking the *direction* of that career, and a reassessment may head you in the right one. It was not her writing that was at fault. When she switched from modern-day romances to historical fiction, she found her real niche. Others I have known have struggled with the same lack of fine-tuning which a complete analysis of their hands and thus their vocational skills would have provided.

You may have spent years studying in a field that is not accentuated on the hand, not realizing that a simple sideways step might turn you toward the success you wish for.

Study the map of the motivational areas of the hand on page 115 then compare this map with the vertical lines on your own finger sections. Remember that they are always more numerous on the bottom sections, and there may be few or none at the tips.

On your handprint, mark how many lines appear on each of the finger sections.

Now you may assess the area of your life in which your own emphasis has been put. Are you finding few lines that do reach into the middle phalanges? If so, you are suffering from the "can't get it off the drawing board syndrome" which means that you have good ideas, but cannot put them into practice.

Are there any fingertips that show clear, straight, vertical lines? If so, these fingers and their three sections show that in these areas you have put forth successful effort, which may pay off in your personal life as well as your job.

Another set of key words you might commit to memory are

Thumb:	I feel
Index:	I do
Middle:	I learn
Ring:	I experience
Little:	I desire

Where is your own effort being put? Do you desire more than you are getting? Do you do more than you desire or want?

Be careful when assessing the vertical lines on fingertips. If

Psychological Relationships

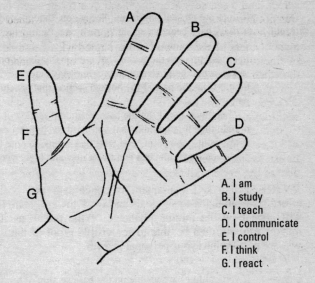

A. I am
B. I study
C. I teach
D. I communicate
E. I control
F. I think
G. I react

they are tilted and at an angle, they are more probably indications of glandular health than achievement lines. See my previous book, *Beyond Palmistry*, for the meanings of these angular lines.

Are there any finger sections that have no vertical lines at all? Check the motivational map on page 115 to see which ones these are and what they may mean to you.

The absence of any vertical lines could mean that you are not putting forth enough effort in that area of your life. This would be of distinct importance in your personal growth as well as in business.

A lack of any lines is like a red flag, warning you that some work must be begun in that area of your inner personality and motivation.

ACTIVITY AND THOUGHT LINES

Thumb
"I will"

If lines are present on the middle section, thought and activity have been occurring in the area of willpower and desire to take control of life. These lines will probably not move up onto the thumb, but are usually found on the lower or middle phalange only. Some may enter the thumb from the part of the bottom section that is actually part of the palm.

If no lines appear on the base or middle section of the thumb, then it is possible that you need to sit down and assess your good points and your bad points, to note the goals you have achieved and to set new and higher goals.

After such a self-assessment is concluded, and positive effort has been made to set goals and work toward them, lines will appear on the middle phalange of the thumb as if by magic. You will then be able to see visible proof of the work you are putting into your personal growth.

Index
"I am"

If vertical lines are visible on the base section of the finger, with some continuing into the middle phalange, then some positive thought and activity has been taking place in the area of self-expression. This finger vitally emphasizes the knowledge of who and what you are, and being satisfied with yourself and your inner growth as a person.

If no lines or only a few are seen on the tip section, then you still have much work to do in learning to know and accept yourself as you are, and in expressing this self to others.

If there are no lines on the finger sections at all, you are possibly a victim of poor self-esteem, or you may have acquired a guilt complex somewhere along the way. If this is the case, setting goals for self-growth and understanding is even more vital, because you must be able to accept yourself before you can accept and communicate with those around you.

It is common to find many more lines on the lowest finger section than are seen on the middle and upper segments. We often wish we would see ourselves as others see us, but a good clear look at the real self can be not only satisfactory, in the sense of self-discovery, but also helpful in setting goals for improvement. If you are able to apply your will to bettering yourself, then lines will appear on the middle and upper portions of the index finger.

Middle
"I study"

If there are lines on the lower section, with some running upward into the middle of the finger, then you have spent some valuable time in learning the lessons of life. This finger is the indicator of your ability to organize your mind and your feelings. It is also important because it shows how well you have put this knowledge into practice. It is the indicator of conscious knowledge of what you do that you feel is right or wrong. In that sense, it stands for your ability to be in touch with your inner conscience.

Lines on this finger indicate that you are aware of your actions and that they can be dealt with. We have all done things we would rather not have done, or would like to have the chance to do over again. Lines on this finger show that you have begun to conquer the part of you that makes this type of mistake.

If there are lines on the top section of the finger, this would indicate some amount of enlightenment, and that you are capable of setting positive goals and working toward them.

If no lines appear on this finger, it would be most unusual. The indication is that you are not in touch with yourself and need to gain some helpful guidance and counseling. Perhaps a session with a professional guidance counselor would be of assistance.

If the process of self-analysis and assessment of what you have learned from life is successful, these lines will begin to appear on the lower phalange and will carry upward into the upper sections of the finger. If you are past midlife, they may

be more numerous on the middle section as they begin to
appear, working slowly toward the tip.

Should this finger be lined from base to tip, you deserve a
well-needed pat on the back, because you have learned from
the lessons of life, and will continue to benefit. It does not,
however, mean that you must no longer set goals and work
toward them.

An involved mind, learning and doing, will resist old age, as
well as prolong the real enjoyments of life and living! Never
cease to learn, as there is always more worth knowing.

Ring finger "I teach"	This finger does not refer to the profession of class-room teaching, but rather how well you can pass on to family, friends, and coworkers what you have learned from life. The finger relates also to how you interact and interrelate with those around you, and whether you have been able to realize your dreams and aspirations or ideals. If there are lines on the finger's lower and middle sections, then you have begun this process. It is normal to have three times as many lines on the lowest finger section, as we have many more chances to do these things than we would ever be able to take advantage of.

Any lines on the tip section represent a life that is
rich in the satisfaction of having shared reward,
achievement, and enrichment with those around us.
They often also indicate projects that have been followed through to successful completion.

It is common to find one or more lines on this fingertip. If no lines have reached the tip, it may be
because of your youth, or perhaps you have not yet
had opportunities to give to others as much as you
would like to give. Should no lines appear on the finger at all, then you are so wrapped up in yourself that
you cannot give.

It is important to remember that our ability to give is always
gauged by what we have to give. A lack of lines on one or more

of the other fingers might shed some light on why no lines appear on this outward-oriented finger.

Once you have begun to break the ice and make progress toward more positive self-growth, it will be easier to give some of what you have learned to others. Everyone has important knowledge gained from experience to offer, but some of us are afraid to offer it for fear that it might be rejected. We remain silent. This is a mistake, for even if you do not believe you are getting through to another, perhaps some small word of encouragement or piece of valuable advice will lodge in the ear of your listener and be remembered when he or she needs it most. Be certain that you always pass on the positive in life and never the negative. Negative input is always less welcome and adds nothing to either your own growth or that of your listeners.

Should you conquer this aspect of repression and begin to freely give of yourself, the action lines will appear on all finger sections very rapidly.

Little Finger: "I communicate"   The littlest finger deals with the deepest needs and desires of the human personality. One of the most critical of these needs is to communicate with others. Although many animal species show both ability and need to communicate, we know little or nothing about what these needs and abilities may be. We do know, however, that only the human has complex means of communicating through eyes, sound, body language, hand motions, writing, singing, dancing, and a host of others. Even the most solitary of us might paint or write poetry to communicate with others. Some of our greatest and most creative minds are better known after their deaths, through the words or works they leave us, a form of silent but lasting communication.

This finger also holds the deep needs and desires of the human spirit. It would be most unusual to find no lines on the base section of this finger, as it would be hard to imagine a human being who has no needs or desires. Normally there are dozens of vertical lines, both faint and bold, upon this bottom finger section, representing these hidden needs.

If there are lines on the middle phalange, it shows that you are making some attempt to assess your own personality and to see yourself as you are, with all your good points and your faults. No positive progress can be built upon a negative root. Positive thinking cannot be learned until you have freed yourself from all negativity. If there are lines on this middle section, you are in the process of releasing that negativity. It is time to learn to work toward a goal.

If lines reach the top, then you may be at the point where your needs and your desires are being realized.

Any lines on this tip section usually represent a culmination.

Most hands will be marked with these upright lines of effort, and the horizontal lines or blocks that represent obstacles to progress may appear on some finger sections as well, showing the places of past or present stress and frustration in the life.

How does this relate to your career? Simply put, if you are able to set a goal and work toward achieving it, then your ability to make progress in all areas of your life will be stimulated. You will be considered a promising employee, no matter what your job, and should you wish to begin reeducating yourself, your teachers and instructors will find you the perfect student—one who wishes to learn.

When you are ready to make that move into a better job, a satisfying career, a larger salary, then the same rules will apply, ensuring that you will reach the top.

How can this be? What magic could make all this happen? The ability to set goals and to achieve them makes you a better person in almost any way you can imagine. A great mind once said, "Whatever the mind of man can conceive—and believe—he can achieve!"

And that is an eternal truth.

SETTING GOALS

Setting goals is not like making a New Year's resolution that you will quickly forget. Setting a goal means reaching for a higher level of one kind or another.

Let's say that you are a truckdriver in training. If you wanted to own a fleet of trucks and make millions, that would be considered pipe dreaming, right?

But what if you were the best and most careful trainee the trucking company ever had? What if you set a goal, a short-term goal to own your own truck within two years' time? Would you be willing to work hard and give up luxuries to own that truck? Would you be willing to take extra little jobs here and there instead of relaxing all weekend? If you can say yes, then you are on your way to understanding how to set a goal!

Short-term goals are goals you can reach within a given period, probably a year or two, perhaps a few more, depending on the end result you desire.

Owning that first truck would be the short-term goal you would reach through hard work, giving up all but necessary spending, and concentrating all your effort on the goal—that truck.

I have seen a beginning pharmacist end up owning a chain of thirteen drugstores. Within a little more than two years he owned the first store. Then he began to work toward the second, and on he went. How? By setting a short-term goal to own the first and learning what it took to attain it.

Some may laugh and say "Well, that's the American dream, after all." It is indeed the American Dream to reach higher than you can presently grasp. But it is not confined to America. The old saying "Cream always rises to the top" may only make sense to those who used to get their milk on the doorstep in

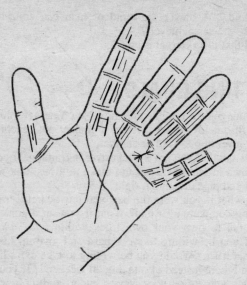

"Effort" lines will appear on the palm under the four fingers, indicating effort in that field. Note the creative "haystack" under the ring finger and the "teacher's square" under the index finger.

glass bottles, but what it means is that your goals and effort will inevitably push you right to whatever you consider the top.

Long-term goals are only a result of achieving several short-term goals in a row, sort of like getting to the World Series. Suppose you were a youngster dreaming of hitting in the Big Leagues. How would you get there? By learning to run, catch, hit, and field so well that everyone would notice you, especially the Big-League scouts. If you can learn to try that hard, you need never fear your effort will not be noticed—and rewarded.

Suppose you were a manicurist dreaming of owning a big cosmetics firm. Out of the question, right? Ask Mary Kay. Ask most of the successful people, men and women, in the business world today. It's not who you know—it's who you *are*.

Learning to work the goal system is not drudgery, it is plea-

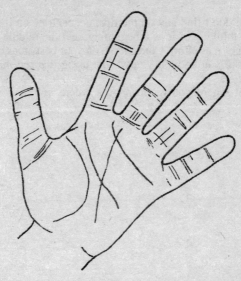

Horizontal lines on the finger sections are "blocks" indicating stopped progress in the area covered by that phalange. The blocks on the thumb tip here represent frustration of one kind or another, often at a lack of progress. But they may represent a personal problem as well as may the ones on the bottom section of the little finger.

sure, pride, and profit. You may have to do with less for a while, or take out a loan to go to the right training facility or school. But every minute will be worth it.

Draw an outline of your hand or use a lightly inked print, and with your magnifying glass look carefully at all your finger sections, especially the middle and the tips. If you see any vertical lines at all, mark them firmly on the drawing or the print. Use a blue or green marking pencil, so that you can see them clearly.

Now, with a red pencil or marker, put in any that you find on the tip sections. Be certain that they are perfectly straight and upright. These represent areas in which you are more likely to continue to achieve.

If you don't find any on the tips, concentrate on the lowest section, thinking of it as a beginning, and the middle section, thinking of it as effort. Concentrate on your best areas of effort, and before you know it you will be using that red marker on every finger.

Forget where you've been—it's where you're going that counts!

8

LINING THINGS UP

The palmar lines on the hand also make a contribution to any vocational analysis.

It should be remembered, however, that these lines do move and change. Some will disappear, while others will appear for the first time. Your hand changes when you change, which is one of the main reasons why palmistry usually fails in making any predictions for the future.

As a child becomes an adolescent and then an adult, his or her hand grows, changes, and may even reflect one shape in childhood then change to another in adulthood. I have never seen a hand change from the action to the emotional or the technical to the emotional, but I have seen most of the other two categories change. My own hand has remained the action type throughout my life, but my youngest son's hand changed from action to technical at age twenty-four. Even the lines on his hands changed when he left his intended profession as a broadcaster to become a sales executive for a building supplies company—a drastic change indeed. The one thing that did not change was the elongated tip on the little finger, which was equally useful for a broadcaster or for someone in sales.

Major Lines

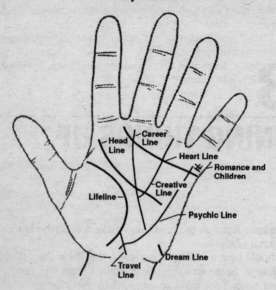

Lines on the palm and fingers do change position, some moving upward and some downward while new lines are often added to the hand. Others may be there one year and gone the next. After the first analysis of your strong points and job skills, you may decide that you will set a goal and reeducate yourself to enter a different field. It would be interesting and instructive for you to take a handprint every three to six months, to discover the changes you will see according to the progress you have made. A running file of your own prints is always interesting, especially when you are in a process of transition, for a good handprint will show this step-by-step progress.

I have a thirty-year file of prints for some people, and many changes can be seen in them over the years. One individual, a man in his late sixties, had had a consuming interest in meditation and healing research, but after fifteen years, he stopped following this interest due to ill health. At that time, the lines between the ring and little fingers on his hand completely disappeared. Within the last eighteen months he has returned to this earlier interest, and the lines in that place are beginning to grow and become visible again.

Lines on the hand can and do change radically from very early childhood to extreme old age.

Here is how you assess them.

HEART LINE

This line is the upper transverse, beginning under the little finger and running toward the middle or index finger.

Chaining of this line is not an indication of any such thing as a troubled love life. It is an indication of problems with teeth, eyes, circulation, and the heart itself.

If the line dips low in the hand, then your personality is geared toward helping others more than yourself. It indicates a lack of one-upmanship. In one sense, a heart line that is very low could be considered a humanitarian indication, and the owner one who thinks of other people first.

Jobwise, such a line would suggest that you would do best in some form of social work or a service profession.

If the low-set line ends on the middle finger, it is a symbol of compassion for others, and that you will never act in a selfish manner. This would fit you well for work in a team situation such as emergency medicine, physical education teacher, 911 operator, ambulance attendant or paramedic, physical therapist, counselor, nursing specialist, or work in a convalescent or retirement home.

If the line ends on the index-finger base, the inclination to help others is still there, but you will be much more useful as a specialist running your own operation or business, where you make the major decisions. Choose such professions as doctor, employment counselor, travel agent, insurance sales, real estate, educator, rehabilitation therapist, and inspirational writer.

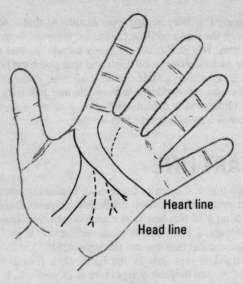

Heart line

Head line

Possible head line forks indicating talent as a writer. Heart line ending on index finger or middle finger shows outward orientation.

If the line ends in a fork or a split that runs in two or three different directions, then both aspects will apply, and almost any profession that offers some sort of service to others, from fireman to sketch artist or color therapist, will be correct.

If a low-set heart line is combined with a strong psychic line, you should do well in any profession where being able to assess others and their needs is an important factor.

A heart line may be judged as low if it is one inch or more below the base of the middle finger. If the hand is very long, of the emotional type, then the heart line may be one and a half or two inches below the flexure line of the index finger.

Some lines begin higher and then dip down across the palmar surface. This indicates a person who may have begun life with a less giving sort of personality, and for whatever reason became the type of person who would cheerfully give you the shirt off his or her back, so to speak.

A heart line that is three-quarter inches beneath the middle finger is in a normal setting, and more emphasis should be placed on where it ends, which indicates whether the owner will be more extroverted or less open and generous.

If the heart line is high set, running close under the base of the fingers, then the subject's instincts are less for service to others and more toward self-expression.

Any job in which you are responsible only for your own actions would be suitable.

If the line ends on the middle finger, then the chosen profession should still be in some area of service to others, either in a direct or an advisory capacity. Jobs would range from caterer or fashion consultant, to limousine driver, airline attendant, or gift shop/florist shop owner.

Interruptions in this line may be health indicators and should not be considered as career directions.

HEAD LINE

This line begins somewhere under the index finger and runs at an angle across the hand. It is the middle transverse line.

This line has been much misunderstood in the past, especially in terms of its length. Normally a short, tight line indicates a high IQ, usually 125 and over. The clearer this line appears, the better the intelligence and the ability to think things through and make decisions. A shorter line may end under the middle finger, but may extend to the area beneath the ring finger. This indicates quick and alert thinking and a good, multitalented intellect.

Career choices for this shorter head line are so wide and varied that you should use the many other career indicators on the hand to choose a direction. Whichever you do choose, you will probably rise rapidly to a higher position.

A longer line, ending under the ring finger or at the edge of the palm, indicates that you are quite intelligent but are more inclined to concentrate on one profession and to follow it throughout life.

This line formation often belongs to the scientist, science technician, computer genius, communications technologist, astronomer, or similar "tech" professional. Working in research or experimental laboratories or programs is just your cup of tea if you have this line, as you enjoy new and innovative projects. Solving mysteries may be part of your job, or might express itself in a part-time hobby of reading or writing detective novels. You should choose one area of science as a start and learn as much about that field of study as possible. You may apply this as a teacher, a professor, or a field researcher. You will constantly be on a quest to enrich your mind.

A head line that drops down across the hand in a deep, downward angle is the mark of the more imaginitive individual. Your outlook on life is not tough or harsh and more likely to be unusual or romantic in some way. You will use creativity and imagination as part of your daily life.

Any profession that allows free use of these abilities will suit you, from any type of art to creating computer games. If you enjoy color and variety, you might find that a job as a designer or costumer for stage, television, or screen will suit. This is also the aspect of the musician or the poet, and a career that includes some creative work in either of these areas may be a suitable choice.

If the head line ends in a fork, then your inclination is to be a writer, whether this is your present job or just a dream you hold dear. If you do not presently have a job that involves writing, it would be a good idea to find time to enroll in some creative writing courses to find where your talents are hidden. Once you find your feet, then you should begin considering a career change. But be certain that you have explored and learned your craft thoroughly, as there are as many untrained writers as there are starving artists in garrets. Writing is an art, but what you write must first be of interest to the reader and appealing to a publisher or magazine editor. Only writers who have learned these things will reach real success in this profession.

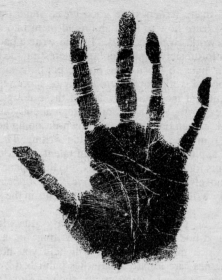

Hand with joined head and life lines. Note the writer's fork on the head line. This woman is a college professor who has had several major books published.

A short head line with a fork that is almost level indicates a writer of fact, such as a reporter, journalist, documentary writer, advertising copywriter, or nonfiction author. If you do write fiction, it will have some solid factual basis, such as the work of Michael Crichton, whose *Jurassic Park* is a science fiction classic, containing real information about DNA, cloning, paleontology, and other scientific fields.

The head line that drops a half inch or more, indicates the writer who works with creative fiction, or historical events around which he or she can build a story. Detective or mystery novels fit here, as does biography. All forms of fiction are open to this medium-set writer's fork. Magazine articles, desktop publishing, newsletters, reports, and script writing are all also possible for this line ending.

Although many writers have good ideas, some training is necessary to learn how to form and mold them into an interesting framework. Everyone says, "I could write a book about my life." Unfortunately, no matter how interesting most people believe their lives to be, it may not be possible to create a saleable piece of work from them. It may be more realistic to write a novel that incorporates many of these things, as it is sometimes easier to write about others than about yourself.

If the fork is seen on a very long, down-drooping head line, it indicates romance, fantasy, and fiction writing. There are a great many applications for this sort of talent, including short stories, scripts for television or movies, and the expanding field of unusual novels such as the recent *Celestine Prophecy*, which is so cleverly written that many think the events in the story are factual.

Several of the science fiction and fantasy greats have had this low head-line fork. Begin your writing for a fantasy "fanzine" which may not pay but will help you hone your skills. "Fanzines" are usually quarterlies published by fans of certain movies or television programs, such as *Star Trek*, *Star Wars*, or *Dr. Who*.

You will find some of these listed in some science fiction price guides. A creative writing teacher may be able to help you find others.

Many writers with this low fork write poems, prose-poems, and musical lyrics. The talents of such people are varied and all that is usually necessary is to learn which of yours is strongest and to train it thoroughly.

Many jobs are open to the person who can write, as any glance through the Help Wanted pages will tell you.

It may or may not be true that writers are born and not made, but there are many writers who have struggled along in some other job a good portion of their lives, only to reach success in middle or old age when they began finally to let their creative juices flow.

CAREER LINE

This line begins either at the center base of the palm or on the outer edge of the lower palm. It used to be known as the fate line, but actually indicates your career directions and changes in what you are doing.

If it begins in the center bottom of the palm, rising generally to the base of the middle finger, you are likely to be a person whose talents lie in a professional field, and whose determination and perseverance will take you to the highest levels. If your line looks this way, then find which area is the best for you and begin reeducating yourself as soon as possible.

There may be interruptions on this line, breaks, splices, or deviations in direction. These will outline a complete picture of your job history from late teenage years to now. Every time you made a job change or a shift in career direction, the line will have changed as well.

Career lines may actually begin on the lower outside portion of the palm, in the area that pertains to imagination. If this is the beginning of yours, then your true career may begin a bit later in life, but whatever job you choose will be creative, perhaps inventive or innovative, and will definitely be a career, as opposed to just a weekly paycheck.

Some hands show an ordinary career line running fairly centrally up the midline of the hand, but at or about the middle transverse or head line, there is a branch or spur line coming in from the area of the imagination. This would show that you had spent the first portion of your life doing whatever job presented itself, or in some boring, dead-end position. Then at thirty, give or take a year, you suddenly realized or discovered your real talents and abilities and made a drastic change in your direction!

Such an indication would be seen if a woman had spent the first ten or twelve years of her life in an office job, and then, whether through inspiration, intuition, or a good vocational analysis, she discovered that she had a talent for art, honed it, and took a job as an artist for a big corporation. In one of my case files I have the print of an ordinary man, a

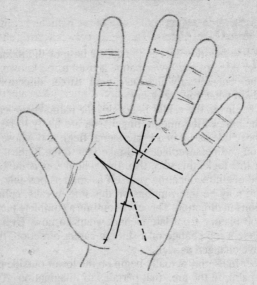

The career line may have several beginnings at the bottom of the hand. Splices indicate career changes. Career line endings can differ widely.

husband and father, who had driven a truck for a local railway express company for fifteen years or more. His hand showed a genius for business and a short, tight head line—a sharp mind. I explained some of this to him and told him he was capable of much more than he had been doing. At the time he seemed amused and puzzled, but within five years he had opened a small restaurant near a large midtown college, with his wife as pizza chef, and within a few short years, he had expanded twice. Today he wears designer shoes and clothing, drives a luxury car, and owns a controlling interest in a chain of very good restaurants! The hand showed that the ability and good business sense were already there, but he had not realized it.

The space on the career line between the head and heart lines covers the years thirty to fifty-five on most hands. Dating events on this line begins at the base of the palm and continues upward toward the fingers. The years between birth and age thirty take up the space from the bottom of the palm upward to the head line.

One some hands, there are a lot of splice lines and line breaks in these earlier years of life. Splice lines are places where two career lines run side by side for an eighth of an inch or so, indicating a gradual change to another field. If the field is not very different from what you were doing, then the line will be very close to the original career line. If you change fields to something totally different, then there may be a wider space between the dual lines. A change such as that described above, from truck driver to restaurateur would be a wide variance. A change from being a librarian to being a novelist would not be too drastic. Nevertheless, a change is a change, and there will be an overlapping area we call a splice to indicate that change.

Within the head to heart line space, these splices would indicate that the career direction changed in midlife, somewhere between thirty and fifty-five, depending on whether the splice is close to the head line's age of thirty or the heart line's marking of age fifty-five.

Above the heart line, the age is fifty-plus. It is not unusual to find dual career lines that continue in this space together all the way up to the base of the fingers. In this case, the individual has either two careers or a single line of work and an absorbing, time-consuming hobby. This would be the case for a talk show host whose consuming passion was speedboating, for instance, or a computer expert whose favorite pastime was building and flying model airplanes.

Some hands show a continuous career line that does not taper off until it reaches the finger flexure line. This is a person who keeps working until he or she reaches the end of life.

A career line that ends under the middle finger indicates a strong affiliation with the world of business and finance. It may mark the individual who owns his or her own business.

If there are no breaks or splices along its length, then you may have been lucky enough to fall into the right career niche fairly early in life and not to have deviated much in your rise to the top.

If the line is deep and strong, then you will indeed reach the top in whatever direction you have chosen.

If the career line bends and swings over to end under the ring finger, then you have at some time or other discovered that you have artistic talent of some kind and changed to a career in that field.

If the career line seems to end at the base of the index finger, you will have chosen a field in the world of media, entertainment, or public service in a highly visual way, such as politics or trial law.

If the career line seems to have split off somewhere near the head line and zooms up to the little finger or the side of the ring finger, it is probably not a career line, but a creative line.

CREATIVE LINE

This line is not a major line, but its influence on your life and your future may have major importance. It belongs to the individual who has basic creativity of some kind and who cannot not use it.

An office worker who spends his or her time drawing and writing whenever the job is not demanding may find that this creativity is an inborn need, not just a way to fill up time. With training, it may lead to a position as editor of a house organ or company magazine, some kind of desktop publishing, or something that is much more creative than the original career.

A plumber who suddenly begins to invent new methods of using valves and pipes may find him or herself head of a large plumbing supply company.

In one case, a man who had this line had been a mortician for fifteen years and suddenly had a brainstorm leading to the development of an entirely new and different way of developing and maintaining cemeteries. In another, a housewife who was a cancer patient suddenly decided that it would be fun to open a shop in the local hospital to sell specialized undergarments, clothing, and wigs for cancer patients, especially wigs for children with cancer, who are on chemotherapy and have lost their hair. This idea could have taken hold and led to a large chain of such special shops had her health allowed her to continue.

These examples illustrate what can be done by an inventive and creative mind.

This line can always be distinguished from the career line as it is usually deep and strong, and shoots straight off the career line at a wide angle upward to the ring or little finger.

If it is on your hand, consider yourself lucky and set out to discover in just which area of creativity or artistic talent your abilities may lie hidden, like a pearl in an oyster.

LIFE LINE

This line begins between thumb and index fingers, just as does the head line, and sweeps downward to the base of the palm, often in a wide curve.

Its length has nothing at all to do with how long or short your life will be. I have seen a life line vanish within three months' time, and yet the owner lived another twenty years or more.

It is the depth and clarity of this line that tells more about the length of your life, or at least whether or not you enjoy your life. The deeper and clearer it is, the better.

The life line has no career indications as such, but often has tiny spur lines that reach out to touch and join the career line, to stimulate it.

There may also be short, sharp lines that jut upward off the life line, indicating periods of your life in which you've made great efforts at improving your situation or your effectiveness.

The life line may be gauged as covering the years from birth to the age of eighty or one hundred. The age of thirty is found at the halfway point. Life lines can be measured with a piece of thread, cut to fit. When folded in half, the measurement of midlife may be marked in the corresponding place on the hand-print.

Note: The earlier years of childhood may not correspond in length to the years of adolescence and adulthood, as the years of preteen life are less eventful. Later life includes more participation in higher education, beginning work, making love or friendship relations, and myriad other happenings. These years take up a much longer space than do those of childhood, which is why dating on the life line has always been so difficult if the basic understanding of the line's meanings are not fully understood.

Past midlife, the space lengthens even more, as these years may be the most productive of all. The best way to measure the line is to find events you know have happened, such as those indicated by the "effort to improve" lines, and mark the age when they occurred. Then you will have a better idea of where you are on the life line. Another age-old method is to wait until you have a fever and then push down on the base of the palm. A red flush will follow the line right to the age at present. You can then mark that exact point on the handprint with a red dot. This red flush effect can be seen on the heart line as well, thus indicating where you presently are on that line.

It is normal to find the life line and head line intertwined over the first inch or so of their lengths. This merely indicates that you were a normally dependent child, looking to close family relationships for guidance. This area is often heavily chained in older persons, due to the many childhood illnesses they underwent. Modern childrens' hands show much less chaining, as innoculations are now given to avert most childhood diseases, such as measles, mumps, typhoid, and the dreaded poliomyelitis.

If this joined aspect continues farther down the life line, it may indicate that you need to cut your apron strings and move away from anyone who is controlling your life. You cannot make clear career moves unless you are free of such control. It is important to take responsibility for your own life, your actions, and your future.

If there is an obvious space between the beginning of your

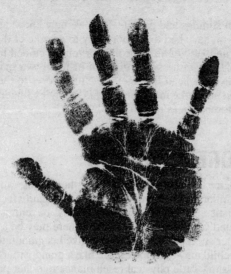

This female hand has a widely separated head line that actually runs up to the base of the index finger and forms part of a teacher's square. This individual is the originator of several new and different areas of research, and has been engaged in teaching them since age twenty-eight. Her career bears no similarity to any of her parents' or ancestors' careers.

head line, and your life line the indication is that you are an independent individual who will always make your own way in life. You may listen to advice, but you will without fail go on to do whatever you feel is right for you—even when it goes against the advice of others. You will balk when anyone tries to overpower or control you.

This indication was at one time regarded as problematic, since it was thought that such independence meant that the owner of such a hand suffered from a lack of the benefits of close family relationships and training in human interaction. This would indeed be a deficit, if that were the true meaning.

This clean and clear separation, however, does not have any such meaning. It is not an indication that one did not love or learn from siblings and parents. It is, we now know, an indication that you have had the opportunity to partake of these relationships and yet not be controlled or totally guided by them.

Those hands with a wide division of these two major lines usually have the head line moving much closer to the area of motivation under the index finger, and the index finger (or ego) may be closer than to the life line itself.

CHILDREN'S HANDS

Although such an individual will show some amount of genetic similarity with parents in traits, personality factors, and characteristics, the child's behavior may be almost totally unconnected with that of the parents. There may be a revision to an earlier ancestor: "Johnny is just like his grandfather, isn't he?" The child may even look more like a grandparent or great-aunt, and show little physical resemblance to either parent.

With this separated beginning, the child may have a separate life of his or her own, vividly imagined. He or she may fantasize about being a prince or princess, captured at birth and raised by a lesser family, never quite conforming. This child may play parts and act out being a superhero, making costumes and elaborate acting-out toys. Today, this young person might be a good customer for computer role-playing games.

SEPARATED HEAD AND LIFE LINES

This separated head and life line complex usually indicates that you may choose a career of an entirely different kind from those chosen by any or all of your immediate ancestors. You will usually make a career of your own, and it will often be based on some kind of inventive or innovative thinking—a whole new field, for instance.

Because of this, you should take time to test your faculties

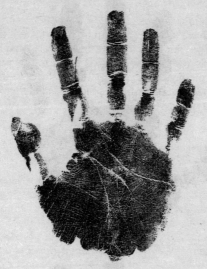

This handprint shows both the effort line on the life line, plus the "wild goose" syndrome.

and aptitudes, as you may begin one career only to change to a more suitable one. Keep your options open.

Joined life and head lines do not have this freedom of choice, and often such people follow a career related in some way to that of their parents, or accept one close to what the parents may suggest.

The widely separated head line indicates that this type of conformity would be the last choice rather than the first. Should this be the case, look at the thumb for frustration blocks, as well as a probable blocking line on the middle section of the index finger, in the area of personal motivation.

TRAVEL LINE

Near the last inch or so of the life line, (higher up if the events occurred earlier in childhood) a sharp line may sudden-

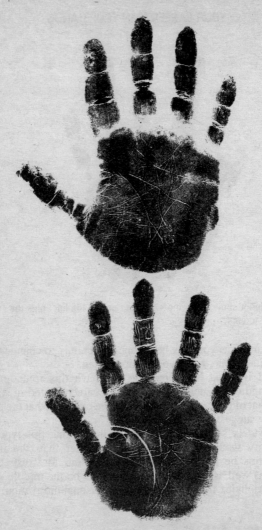

These two hands are children whose first trips were taken before the age of two and a half. At three, both had been taken from America to Europe, to live on a U.S. military base for three years. Note the travel line even on such young hands.

ly break away and run downward at a steep angle toward the center of the palm's base. It usually does not end upon or touch any other major line.

Known as the wild goose syndrome, this is the travel line. If you have it on your palm, it indicates, among other things, that you are the type of person who likes to travel, either as a part of your job, or just for recreation.

Many people who have taken a job that does involve this sort of travel will grow the line, whether or not they enjoy traveling. Found on a young hand, it is an indication that time may be spent in a country other than that in which the child was born. It may also indicate that the child will enjoy moving around from place to place throughout his or her life. If the

This is the hand of one of the children from page 162 fourteen years later. In that time she traveled to most countries in Eastern Europe, during a second three years on the U.S. base. Shortly after this print was taken, she began the first of several trips from the east coast to live in California. Note the extreme length of the travel line. She should seek a job that will allow her to continue this freedom of movement.

child does spend some years in another country, or move permanently to that place, then the line will become longer, clearer, and deeper.

If you're an adult who has this line, home to you may be just the place you hang your hat, as the saying goes, and you will find it hard to build roots in any one place. This spur line may be an indication that you should put some effort into looking for a job that will include a certain amount of travel on business, such as airline work, import/export, or some position with a multinational corporation.

This line is being found more often as the globe shrinks and international travel becomes a daily routine. I estimate that it will become an even more familiar part of many hands as interglobal travel becomes extraglobal, into space.

PSYCHIC LINE

The majority of hands have at least some faint portions of this line running along the outside of the palmar surface.

The clearer the line, and the longer it is, the more likely you are to have some amount of talent for what is known as ESP, or extended sensory perception. This is not a "sixth sense," nor is it second sight, but simply our ability to know things sometimes without being able to explain how we know. In my many years of research into the mind, I have not found anyone who did not have at least a little of this ability, which they could be trained to use more fully. It appears on the hands of good Catholics, members of fundamentalist religions, Jews, Buddhists, and Mohammedans alike. It has nothing whatsoever to do with your philosophy or your religion.

If you find this line on your hand, you need not consider becoming a gypsy fortune-teller or buying a crystal ball. What it does mean is that you have a natural aptitude for knowing or sensing things about people, places, or events, without knowing how you know, such as knowing who is calling when the telephone rings. It is not important how this ability works, only that you learn to use it and respect it.

Career options:

Family counselor	Psychologist
Vocational counselor	Psychiatrist
Police or law enforcement	Motivational trainer
Lawyer, judge	Sports coach or personal
Sales	trainer
Sales manager	Minister, priest, rabbi
School counselor	Talent agent
	Supervisor

There are many ways in which this sensitivity can be utilized to make your life run more smoothly, and your career direction maintain a steady rise upward.

If you have this line, you need not use it knowingly, but you will find, like most people, that it operates on its own. All of our inborn abilities are given us to use for ourselves and for others. This one can be of great benefit both to yourself and those around you.

DREAM LINE

This line is not a major line in essence, but it does indicate that you have an active subconscious mind. Those who have it usually dream many times during sleep, and usually can remember at least one of these dreams. The line also indicates that you probably dream in color, whereas most of the human race dreams in black and white only.

Vocationally, this line might give you the ability to use dreams deliberately, perhaps in problem-solving. If you will go over a problem thoroughly before you sleep, and firmly believe that something you dream will help to solve the problem, you can train yourself to retrieve it.

Dream lines sometimes belong to those who do not remember their nightly dreams but are likely to spend some time each day daydreaming.

Solutions to problems may be gained in this way just as they might be in sleep.

No matter how you use it, this line indicates that you have an active imagination, and you should seek a job where imagination is useful and welcome.

Careers:

Inventor	Advertising
Computer programmer	Printing
Systems Analyst	Art
Designer	Music
Fashion	Literature
Computer game inventor	

The romance and children area of the hand has no application to vocational analysis. For explanation of what it does mean, please read my previous book.

BOOSTERS

Under each of the four fingers, there may be a marking or two that will be useful in determining career directions and how well you are able to apply them. They act as a kind of "booster" when they are visible on the handprint.

THE TEACHER'S SQUARE

This mark is a square form that is located under the index finger. It is composed of four separate lines and contains a square somewhere in this pattern. These squares occur in various sizes, large and small, but all have the identical meaning. If one of these squares does appear under your index finger, then you have the ability to guide others by good advice or counsel.

You may also have the ability to break down complicated information into its basic components and explain them to others so that they understand them easily. Such a talent is unusu-

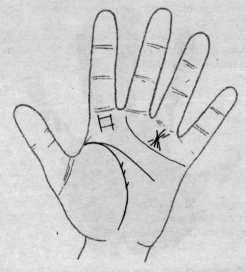

Effort lines coming from life line. "Booster" lines under fingers may include teacher's square and creative "haystack."

al and would be invaluable in many job situations, as well as in dealing with children in any way.

Career choices:

Teacher	Adult education
Youth leader	Specialist instructor
Tutor	Flight school trainer
Mechanical instructor	Supervisor
Television documentary writer	

There are many people who have learned to understand and become familiar with extremely complicated systems and mechanisms, from computers to crafts, automobile repairs to carpentry. If you are one of these people, any special knowledge you have gained may be boring and dull to you. To a novice, however, what you consider boring may be fascinat-

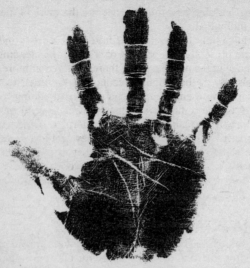

This action-mental blended hand is that of a young research-oriented doctor. Note the teacher's square under the index finger. He will eventually
become an instructor in his specialty.

ingly intricate. If you find the teacher's square on your hand, it
will be natural for you to pass on the ideas and knowledge you
possess to someone else.

If there are just vertical lines under this finger, and no square
formed at all, then you are working at bolstering and using
your own self-esteem. You may have taken on a job that
involves speaking in public, acting, or in some way using basic
authority. These lines signify ambition and effort being
expended.

LINES UNDER MIDDLE FINGER

Lines under this finger are usually formed when the owner
is studying something new. They can also be found on the
hands of those who may have adequate formal education, but

cannot stop learning new things. They are the mark of the self-educated individual.

If you have only one or two of these lines, it may indicate that you are presently in a process of self-analysis leading to a career change in the near future. If there are three or more, then you are already at the point of reeducating yourself to make such a change or to enrich what you are already doing.

I have seen many handprints that showed several of these lines, and when I explained what they meant, the owners would look surprised, smile, and tell me that they had just gone back to college or into some special classes that would add to their present knowledge. It's a safe bet that if you have these lines you will never be satisfied in a dull, repetitious job for any length of time!

"THE HAYSTACK"

Under some ring fingers there may be a wide spread of vertical lines, or just one or two. What is usual is a sort of fan made up of three or four lines, narrowing in and then spreading out again a half inch below where they started. These lines represent creativity.

Near the heart line they indicate creative ideas or talents. In the middle area between the heart line and the base of the finger, they represent gathering of tools and initiative that will allow you to use the idea creatively. Near the finger base they indicate acting upon the idea itself, actually doing something with it.

This set of steps is the one-two-three of accomplishing anything creative. First you must have a new and creative idea. Second, you must equip yourself to carry it through. Third, you must begin to use the equipment and to follow through to a conclusion.

Naturally we all have more creative ideas than we will ever use. This is why there is a fan of lines at the base of the finger and a narrowing in in the midsection indicating that they are not all being acted upon. There may be fewer than half when they fan out again, since few of us ever get to act upon all our new ideas.

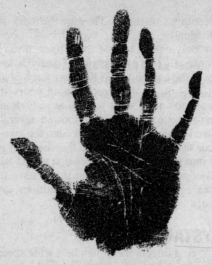

This thirty-five-year-old woman has a career change coming up. Her employment as an office worker is not suitable for her abilities. Note the writer's fork on the head line, and the creative "haystack" under the ring finger.

If there is just the fan at the bottom of the finger, with the narrowing in bundle of lines and none coming out again, then you may have lots and lots of good ideas you cannot use because you are not in the right job.

If this is the case, then a careful analysis of the hand should be done, and an aptitude study made, to determine where you might best utilize this creativity. When you have made a decision, get into the proper education or retraining course and allow your creative urges to flower in a new job.

Career choices:

Art   Jewelry-making
Crafts instructor   Television
Magazine or newspaper writer   Rehabbing older houses

Author   Interior decoration
Dressmaker   Paint or wallpaper specialist

LINES UNDER LITTLE FINGER

These vertical lines indicate an ability to understand and utilize money well, an essential practicality.

If you have these lines, you can consider any job where knowing how and why money "works" would be useful.

Careers

Real estate developer   Buying and selling real
Stock market broker   estate
Commodity broker   Banking industry
Any form of accounting,   Insurance industry
  CPA, IRS, etc.   Owning a rental agency
Commercial properties specialist   Business owning

LINES BETWEEN RING AND LITTLE FINGERS

If these are present, then you have the mark of the "Healer," and any job that has some connection with the health industry would be suitable.

Choices:

Nurse, licensed practical nurse,   Lab technician
Nurse assistant   Research medicine
Hospital work   Biotechnology
Clinic work   Bioengineering
Pharmacist   Physical therapist
Chiropractor   Speech therapist
Doctor

All of these lines and specialized markings on the handprint are of use to you, since they can and do tell you much about your natural career aptitudes and vocational abilities. Make a list of what these indications, then, on the blank outline at the end of this chapter, and sketch in the lines and special marks.

Practice Sheet

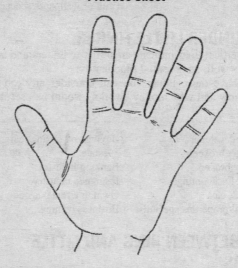

Use a pencil, as some of these indicators may move or change in the next few months and will have to be redrawn.

Remember, when you change, the lines on your hand will also change. If you are making progress, the additional lines and markings on the palm will indicate this.

9

PROBLEMS ARE WHERE YOU FIND THEM

As we discussed in Chapter Three, most hands have a number of effort and activity lines running upward on the fingers, from base to fingertip.

There may also be horizontal lines crossing the fingers. Like horizontal depressions on the fingernails, which represent emotional shock or trauma, such lines across fingernails sections show where a change has been made or some event has occurred that caused problems and stress in your life.

These lines are referred to as "blocks." They often represent a blocked effort, and all of the nice vertical lines may stop when they reach it.

Sometimes there will be many effort lines below such a block and fewer above it. This represents an interruption in the efforts indicated by that finger section.

Blocks may appear on any finger section, and each block affects not only that section, but the other phalanges above it as well, just as a problem in your lower back makes your upper back hurt, too, as it tries to compensate for the problem below.

Psychological Relationships

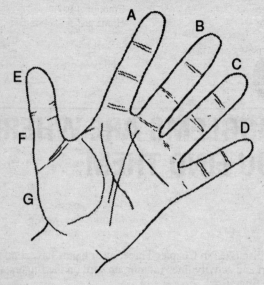

A. I am
B. I study
C. I teach
D. I communicate

E. I will
F. I feel
G. I respond

KEY WORDS FOR FINGERS AND SECTIONS:

Index finger:	I am	I do
Middle finger:	I study	I learn and grow
Ring finger:	I teach	I experience
Little finger:	I communicate	I desire
Thumb:	I will	I feel and react

INDEX FINGER SECTIONS:

Tip:	Advancement
Middle:	Ambition, motivation
Bottom:	Self-esteem

MIDDLE FINGER SECTIONS

Tip:	Organizational ability
Middle:	Emotional balance
Bottom:	Home and possessions

RING FINGER SECTIONS

Tip:	Ability to give
Middle:	Ideals
Bottom:	interacting with others

LITTLE FINGER SECTIONS

Tip:	Communicative ability
Middle	Self-analysis
Bottom:	Urges, needs, sex

THUMB SECTIONS

Tip:	Will to progress
Middle:	Intuition and control
Bottom:	Concern and worry

These are the most important areas of the human personality. There are some important areas on the palm as well, but blocks here are much harder to detect.

If there is a clear, deep line cutting right through the block and continuing upwards into the next finger section, then some effort has been made to overcome the event or trauma that caused the block in the first place.

Some ethnic groups have blocks on all their middle finger sections, apparently due to difficulties in their acceptance by the rest of society.

INDEX FINGER

It is common to have a block on the middle section of the index finger. This is the phalange of ambition, goals, and the urge to grow and achieve.

The most common cause for this block is that your ambition

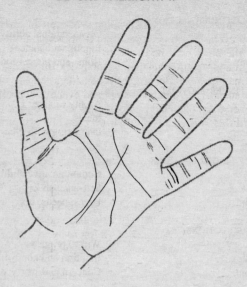

Blocks

Horizontal lines on the finger sections are ``blocks'' indicating stopped progress in the area covered by that section. The blocks on the thumb tip represent frustration of one kind or another, often at a lack of progress, but they may represent a personal problem as well. Blocks on the lower section of the little finger may indicate a problem in the area of sexuality. A half block on the middle of the little finger may indicate a sensitivity to ulcers. It should be watched.

or your career direction was stopped somehow. Often this is because a family financial problem caused you to discontinue your education, and so stopped your progress toward your chosen career.

The closer to the base of this finger section you see the block, the earlier in life this progress-stopping event or circumstance occurred.

A young man or woman may instinctively know that his or her talents and desires suit a certain profession. In spite of this, family pressures, financial problems, or even an early marriage may prevent the proper education from being attained. In this case, the block will be closer to the flexure line between the bottom and middle phalange of the index finger.

In many cases, after a careful consideration of your hand, a block such as this can be blurred and eventually broken up and removed from the hand by beginning your progress once more toward the career you should have been able to pursue in earlier years.

There is no career goal that cannot be resumed in later life, no matter what your age. Within the past several years I have heard numerous stories of persons in their eighties graduating from college and standing proudly with broad smiles of accomplishment beside grandchildren in their twenties. This is an extreme, of course, but if that college degree was once that important to you, or represents a doorway into the career you wanted so badly, take that step and enroll the very next semester and get started!

It is uncommon to find a block on the tip of this finger. Blocks on the lowest finger section represent a situation in which you felt powerless or unable to assert yourself to any extent. Such a block can be overcome by realizing how it came about and not allowing this sort of event to occur in your life again.

MIDDLE FINGER

Blocks on this finger are common when there is a crisis in some area of life.

Blocks on the lowest section are often seen when the home or family is broken up through divorce, accident, or other sudden, irrevocable change. Although many parents do not take their children's trauma into account when divorce is unavoidable, these blocks or trauma lines can and do appear, even on the hands of the very young.

A fire, flood, hurricane, or any other event that upset the home and family situation will also cause these blocks. The closer to the exact base of the finger, the earlier this event took place.

Events in the far past become blurred and faint, yet they show up on the print because they mark the deeper portions of the mind and the personality forever.

Blocks are most frequent on the middle section, the seat of emotional balance. They may be caused by a permanent event such as the death of a beloved family member, or less deep trauma lines could appear temporarily when a friendship breaks up, a romance or marriage ends, or even if a special pet suddenly dies, although that is rare.

It is rare *not* to find a block on this middle finger section. Blocks here represent shocks to a person's emotional balance. A large number of blocks might represent a person whose emotional balance has been constantly upset.

If you have one or even several of these trauma blocks on this section, you will find that making a positive effort to overcome whatever emotional trauma they represent will be rewarding.

It is most unusual to find a block on the tip of the middle finger. A tiny portion of the fingertip might consistently remain blank when the finger is printed. This may be at the tip or on the sides. We call this a "shark bite" as it represents a much less severe problem in the area of career or profession, and might indicate the loss of a job or something similar. It is not an ongoing situation, however, and so does not form an actual block.

Such "shark bites" can appear on any finger section, even within the skin patterns themselves. They represent the same problems a block would indicate, but of much shorter duration. Also, when the problem has been corrected, the "shark bite" disappears, and the entire finger section is seen without empty spaces or whiteouts. (See page 211.)

RING FINGER

Blocks are not uncommon on this finger, but are usually found on the middle section, the place of ideals, aspirations, and dreams. An idealist living in today's world will probably be unable to escape having one or more solid blocks on this finger section. A large number of these would perhaps indicate that he or she would prefer to live in an ivory tower and escape the hurly-burly of the outside world.

A block on the lowest section might be associated with another block in the same place on the bottom of the middle finger, echoing the loss of a lover or dear family member. This finger section refers to interpersonal relationships and friendships, so a block here might indicate a marital problem in the past or the present.

The hand is unable to differentiate between an actual, legal marriage and a longtime relationship, because marriage is technically only a piece of paper, a legal document. A relationship of mutual love and respect that lasts over a long period of time will have the same weight as marriage, and its breakup will cause the same trauma.

A block on the middle finger section represents some event or circumstance that hurt the idealistic urge of the normal human. Losing something upon which one has set his or her heart will cause the same block.

Blocks on the tip section of the ring finger represent problems in working with others in some way related to your ability to help them. It is your wish to give of your time and your self that is being blocked, and this creates a trauma line. A teacher who is leaving the profession because he or she is considered too old to teach might develop such a line. Whatever its strength, it represents an imbalance in your ability to give to others.

LITTLE FINGER

Blocks on the little finger are common on the base and middle sections.

Blocks on the base section may indicate some problem in the area of sexuality. Some blocks appear when a person is undergoing stress in a love relationship or a marriage and when the problem is affecting events in the bedroom.

A problem may arise from too much sexual activity, not enough sexual satisfaction, or some other area of the human sexuality factor. It may also indicate some other problem relating to basic human need. Vocationally, it could refer to being the subject of some type of sexual harassment in the workplace.

A block here could refer to declining sexual urges and a corresponding feeling of inadequacy. If this is the case, an appointment should be made with a sexual dysfunction clinic. A simple course of treatment will no doubt solve the problem.

Ignoring a problem in this area could be a serious mistake, and if there are blocks on this area of your little finger, you should do all you can to discover what is causing them and what may be done to solve the problem. Your needs are **not** being fulfilled.

Blocks in the middle section usually indicate that there is a problem in your ability to analyze your own actions or personality. Some blocks indicate that you are suffering from guilt, although there may be no real cause for such feelings. In some families, a child can be made to feel guilt for natural feelings and reactions. In adult life he or she may hope to have conquered these feelings. The early marks of blocks may remain throughout life, however, especially if the block is very close to the finger flexure line.

A block that enters the middle section from the ring-finger side and does not entirely cross the section but stops halfway or two-thirds of the way across, is not a block but an indication that there is a sensitivity to ulcer in the body's chemistry.

Medical science has now shown that ulcers are not always caused by worry and stress. They are often caused by some virus that initiates the ulcerating process. This block could indicate that your own body is sensitive to this virus and that you should keep a careful watch on your digestive system.

If this deep line appears to be red and angry-looking on the bare hand, then you should consult a physician and ask to be checked for early indications of ulcers.

Stress ulcers may be a result of family, marital, or job stresses, and sometimes a combination of all of these. Such stresses may not by themselves eat through to the point of ulceration, but they may make you sensitive to the virus that does cause ulcers. This type of block is, unfortunately, quite common.

Other blocks on this phalange may indicate some problem in your personal view of what you are doing.

Blocks on the tip phalange are not common, but are seen occasionally. They indicate that there is a problem in communication. This problem may exist in a marriage or love relationship, or in other areas. If the block appears on your hand, then it is time to reassess your ability to talk to others and to communicate your needs fully. A problem here could lead to other and more serious problems. If a man or woman has no one with whom to share his or her deepest feelings and insights, a communications block is formed not only in the life, but also on the fingertip. The longer this problem goes on, the more apparent the block will be.

In a job situation, you may feel that you are not being given enough to say in some way. If this lasts over a long period of time, the block will appear on your hand.

The block usually appears at or about the center of the space from flexure line to the little finger's end. This would be the period of your most productive life, the mid to late twenties and the thirties. If your communication is stifled during this time, it may take years to reassert yourself.

Should a block already be there, it is important to be careful in choosing a love partner to whom you can talk and communicate fully. If this is not done, you will be almost literally starving for someone with whom you can communicate. Intimate communication is one of the deepest human needs.

This finger represents what Freud called the ID, which is the area of our child mind, which often craves things it should not have. Most of us spend our entire adult lives suppressing unwelcome or unsuitable, sometimes illegal, desires. Some rare individuals are in control of this portion of the self from childhood and find it no trouble, not even noticing those unwelcome desires.

A block on this finger is more serious in many ways than a

block on any other finger section, as it represents some very important portions of *you*.

THUMB

Blocks on the base section of the thumb are hardly recognized as such, as there are usually so many of these. Early in my career in learning about hands I heard these lines referred to as "worry lines." Whether they represent worries or not, they do represent concern about some area of the life and so are often numerous.

These lines fan out from the base of the middle section of the thumb, most of them touching the life line. If they end there, they represent basic concerns about life.

If they reach through the life line and the end of the head line, they indicate periods of deep concern, usually about some decisions made or a direction taken. Now and then we may feel that some of our actions are irrational, yet we go on with them. This would cause such a concern line.

In rare cases, the indication may be that you are so overly concerned about something that you fear for your sanity if whatever is bothering you does not stop. This would be a clear and deep concern line, ending exactly on the head line. They are not common, fortunately, as most of us are able to weather the storms of life without real damage. This concern line would only be considered dangerous if the head line were of the low, sloping, long type that droops downward toward the bottom of the palm, with distinct bends in the index, ring, and little fingers.

Should the concern line run clear across the middle and end on the career line, then the concern is about your job. It is common for those who are in a dead-end job or who are unhappy with their employment to have this concern line. In fact, if no change is made, these concern/career lines can be repeated several times down the length of the career line.

Should this be the case, it is certainly time for you to consider making a move, just as soon as you can retrain yourself to do so.

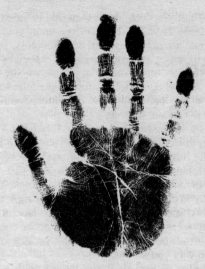

Concern lines mark this male palm from thumb to major lines

Should the concern line run upward across the palm all the way to the heart line, then the concern is for some emotional relationship or situation in which your emotions are involved. This might include having a job where you are not able to deal with or get along with a coworker, even a supervisor or your immediate boss, for whatever reason.

If the concern line is of this type, then it is important for you to get some counseling as fast as you can. It may be that you yourself are completely innocent, and all of the problems and irritations are coming from another person, yet you are being affected to the point where you develop a concern line shooting right across the entire hand! Seek guidance and counseling, from a professional or your minister, priest, or rabbi. If you cannot solve this problem with time and thought, then it is wise to begin the process of changing your company, if not your career!

If the concern line runs right up past the heart line and into the area of family and children, then this is the source of the concern. It may have no direct effect upon your job, but if things at home are not going well and smoothly, your job performance will not be at an optimal level, especially if there are stresses on the job, too. (And what job has *no* stresses?)

These stress and concern lines form one of the largest sets of markings on the palm and are of correspondingly serious importance if they are present.

If there is a strong line with a sharp L-bend at its beginning near the top third of this lowest thumb section, it is known as the "intensity line" and marks you for one of those people who feel things intensely. It is also an indication that you will be intense about doing things and wanting things. You may be impatient if you cannot get a problem solved *right now, please*; and if you become a business owner, supervisor, or boss at any level, you must remember this trait and practice counting to ten before you blow your top when an employee does not handle a situation the way you would.

You will also be impatient and intense with yourself, and usually will not demand perfection from an employee or subordinate when you would not demand the same from yourself. That is one of the good, harmonious things about the intensity line.

With this line you should remember that you are sensitive to blocks and problems being thrown in your way, and learn to take them more gracefully.

You will have to be more accepting of others, not requiring that you understand them before accepting them, for the path to true wisdom leads through accepting—then understanding!

In this life there are many things we cannot understand, not to mention other people we cannot understand. If we let ourselves become vulnerable by insisting on understanding every one of these before we accept it or them, then our progress may be retarded or stopped, and we will never learn the way of true wisdom.

Blocks on the middle thumb section indicate that there is a war going on between your logic and your intuition. That small voice inside you is saying, "hey wait, this may be the wrong thing to do" or the wrong way to go or whatever. You must learn to listen to this voice, for it is the voice of your intuition, and consider what it feels before you plunge ahead and do whatever you're being warned about.

Sometimes we listen, and sometimes we do not, which is why most of us have these horizontal blocking lines about the second section of the thumb.

Once you've learned to let intuition warn you about a wrong decision or course of action, you'll find fewer lines and much more peace of mind.

For this reason this thumb portion stands for control. It expresses the ability to feel when we are going wrong, or turning in a right direction.

Blocks on the tip section of the thumb show that we are frustrated in some way. Either we are frustrated by some sort of nonperformance that can be identified by the blocks on other finger sections, or we are frustrated by lack of progress in some other way, such as a job. If a strong horizontal block appears on one other finger phalange, check to see if it does correspond to your job action.

A good study of the concern lines might show where some of this frustration is coming from. If not, make an assessment of blocks on other finger sections, or lack of effort lines on the fingers.

There are often no activity or effort lines on the thumb's tip, especially if the hand belongs to someone who has been content to take what life dealt him or her and made no effort to assume control. The thumb tip's meaning is will and willpower. If you let someone else control your life, or never gather the strength to do this for yourself, then the thumb's tip will wither and become flabby and flattened looking.

A highly padded, firm, and resilient thumb tip marks the person who has taken control of him or herself and of life.

It takes will to have power.

10

BENDS IN THE ROAD

Some hands have fingers that are strong and straight. A straight finger indicates that the portion of your personality represented by that finger is in good shape. Bends in the fingers indicate that personally and professionally you are in a less than acceptable psychological position.

Finger bends are temporary, for the most part, lasting for a few months or a year or two, until the problem is resolved.

A finger that stays bent, however, indicates an area that needs thought and work to resolve the problem it represents.

A key finger on the hand is the little finger. If it is not only straight, but also spread out, well away from the ring finger, this is an indication that you are an independent person with the ability to control and overcome most of the problems that will arise in your life. A strong little finger can boost a hand that has other problems, and the strength of character represented by the very straight little finger can solve most or all of them.

PSYCHOLOGICAL BALANCE

CONSCIOUS MIND—RADIAL SIDE

In some hands, there is an enlargement of one side or the other. The fingers may be larger or longer and even the palm may be longer on that side.

If this enlargement is toward the thumb side of the hand ("radial" refers to the arm bone on the thumb side), the balance is toward the conscious mind, and the pressure of daily events will determine decisions and reactions. The senses are keen and the reactions fast. This side of the hand is self-willed and may be somewhat egocentric, if this enlargement is extreme.

Although this type of individual is capable of love and concern, he or she is impulsive, and these feelings may not last a lifetime.

Career directions will be toward executive levels or ownership of a business.

SUBCONSCIOUS MIND—ULNAR SIDE

Enlargement on the outer or subconscious side of the hand ("ulnar" refers to the arm bone on the little finger side of the hand) is not as frequently seen.

Those whose ring and little fingers are dominant, however, tend to have a slower approach to life and living, preferring to savor experience and to store it in the memory.

Their efforts are geared toward their fellow man and working toward the greater benefit of all. They love deeply and usually for life.

These people tend to pick careers in which they can work as part of a team, or if working alone, they may prefer research or exploration in some unknown area of science or the arts.

They are often teachers, and have a compulsion to share what they have learned.

The psychological indications of the fingers are

Index: Ego (who we think we are)
Middle: Superego (conscience) (who we really are)

Ring: Persona (mask we wear to show the world)
Little: Id/libido (what we want for ourselves)
Thumb: Character

It is rare to find the middle finger bent, but not quite as rare to find the others bent. "Bent" means a visible curving inward toward a second finger, with the tip at the top of this curve. The finger is not actually bent at an angle, it is just not straight and strong-looking.

All of the other fingers on the hand may lean toward the

Psychological Balance

Conscious Mind   **Subconscious Mind**

Alert   Thoughtful
Aware   Imaginative
Responsive   Creative
Reactive   Introspective
Fast Perception   Intuitive
Outgoing   Socially
In Control   Conscious
Leadership   Daydreamer
Initiative   Artistic
Creative   Concerned
Practical   Empathetic
Compassionate

Logic

Instinct

Significant bends in the fingers in either direction indicate which area is dominant and which is recessive.

middle finger. This indication would be that the personality is still unformed and dependent upon some inner strength for support.

This particular hand might also belong to someone who has suffered a trauma such as sexual molestation, physical assault, or abuse.

In these cases, the basic parts of the personality have suffered a blow, reducing pride, self-esteem, interpersonal relationships, and other major human attributes to an attitude of self-protection. The middle finger represents our most basic strength and our higher self. When all fingers are bent toward this one, it is almost as if they were hiding behind it, looking for protection from what happened to them.

I have seen the hand of a young child who was involved in a particularly gory auto accident with the fingers bent in this way. She had also developed a fear of the dark, insisting on sleeping with a light on.

My advice to her mother was to allow her to have the light, and to let her sleep in her parents' bed for a few weeks, until the trauma's marks on her subconscious mind were erased.

This advice was followed, and, amazingly, the fingers returned to normal straightness within seven weeks.

In an adult, such finger bending may be a temporary thing, or if the problem has existed over a long period, the fingers may take years to straighten out, even when the psychological scars have apparently healed.

In an employment or career situation, it is quite likely that a hand that shows this crippling formation might also cripple the owner, preventing him or her from being able to make a decision to change jobs, or to enter some type of school or training system.

If your hand shows this fear syndrome, it might be worth your while to give some thought to what caused the original fear to arise. If you can discover this, you can conquer it and go on.

Unfortunately, some of these traumas go back to early childhood, and no matter how hard we think, we cannot remember

Psychological Relationships of Fingers

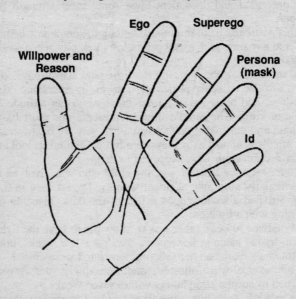

them. In this case, it may be better not to force recall without professional help.

In some rare cases, bent fingers of this type may be caused by osteoarthritis, but normally under those circumstances all fingers will be bent in the same way, including the middle finger.

INDEX FINGER BENT

This can be considered a possessive indication, especially if the fingertips are loosely curved inward toward the palm.

It may represent an overall smoldering resentment that could affect your attitude toward other people, and might cause you

Motivational and Psychological Areas of the Hand

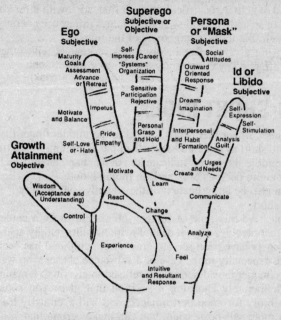

to seek some type of employment where you need not interact too closely with anyone else.

Here again, this attitude may have stemmed from some forgotten childhood event. An attempt should be made to try to find the original event that fostered your resentment.

Perhaps the best way to overcome this problem is by deliberately choosing a profession where helping others is the focal point of the job.

In addition, I would suggest volunteering some time at a hospital, veterans' home, or community function such as the local telethon-involved Ambassadors organization.

Forcing yourself outward into a giving situation can often remove the problem and return you to being the type of considerate and caring individual you were meant to be. Even if this kind of activity is difficult to do at first, stick with it for six months or so and you will see a tremendous difference not only in yourself, but in the straightness of the finger.

Choosing a career that involves lots of contact with other people offers a key opportunity for you to grow.

TOO-SHORT INDEX

An index finger that bends inward to the middle finger that is also so short as to be no longer than the beginning of the tip on the middle finger can indicate an ethnic characteristic, as it is common to persons of American Indian blood.

It can also be an indication of the addictive personality if it is very short.

If you have this type of finger, you should make a career choice that involves a great deal of responsibility. Oddly, these short fingers have been seen to grow after adulthood has been reached, especially in the case of a substance abuser who was able to conquer the addiction and refused to give in to it again.

By deliberately choosing a position that gives you some responsibility for good performance, and will eventually lead to even more self-possession, you can make certain that your inner strength and self-control will grow on a continuous basis. After a period of such strengthening activity, the finger will straighten out, and in some cases will actually grow in length by an eighth to a quarter of an inch.

With either of these indications, career choices might be

Entertainer	Messenger or parcel delivery
Office manager	Media trainee
Supervisory assistant	Physical therapist
Cinematographer	Emergency medicine
Photojournalist	Ambulance attendant
Business manager	911 operator
Stock market clerk	Police dispatcher
Post office worker	

If you have either the bent or too-short finger, you should choose a job that bolsters your self-approval. Deliberately putting yourself in a position of cooperating with others and offering them assistance and aid will counteract any introvertive tendencies you may have.

In a short time you will have forgotten that you were ever any different. The finger will show that.

RING FINGER BENT TO MIDDLE FINGER

Ring fingers may be bent either to the inside of the hand, or the outside edge.

If the ring finger leans at the tip toward the middle finger, you may have been forced into trying to be someone you really are not. This is usually done by someone else—perhaps a spouse or parent, but rarely a good friend. In reaction to this, rather than resist, you may have taken the easier path and "bent" to someone else's desire. The bending finger shows this clearly.

You can offset this by assessing just what you have been allowing to happen, and then taking a stand against any further pressure from outside individuals. It is acceptable to challenge yourself, but it is not acceptable to allow others to push you in directions you do not want to go.

The intelligent way to handle such a situation is to seek some good psychological counseling through a religious or family service organization. A motivational counselor might also be a good choice, and even a Dale Carnegie course would be of assistance in helping you see clearly what you have allowed to be done to you.

The finger is bent because you have buried your perceptions and personality and are attempting to identify yourself as just what this other person or persons feel you should be. It is going to take some solid thinking to solve this, once you are able to admit that it has occurred.

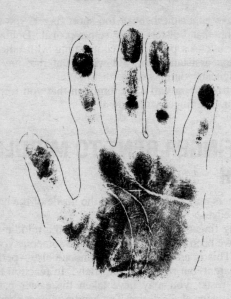

This print is of a twenty-four-year-old male, of the technical type, it shows the electronics skin pattern under the ring and little fingers. The dropping head line, however, indicates lack of motivation, echoed by a short index finger and bends in the index, middle, and ring fingers. The subject has no foundation or identity of his own. Only the ring finger is almost straight. Note the sports thumb, offset to the hand.

Due to this pressure, you may even have chosen a career in which you are unhappy and ill placed, just because this is what your parents wanted you to do, just as the young woman I described in the introduction did. In her case, it was not too late. She was still in college, and by adding an extra summer semester, the changeover to dramatic arts was accomplished. If she had gone on to a job as a librarian, she would have been miserably unhappy. Her mother had been a librarian all her life and enjoyed it thoroughly. But for her daughter it was wrong.

It is not healthy for a parent or any other authority figure to force a career on someone who may be highly talented in his or her own natural field.

If this has happened to you and you are not now in college, you will probably have to locate some financial assistance and find a local college offering the courses you need to make a change. You might find, as have others, that some of the credits you've accumulated will be counted in the new field as well. People at your campus counseling service will discuss this fully with you and direct you to the proper persons to help accomplish such a change.

If you are in this position, and never attended college at all, the first step is to get a Graduate Equivalent Degree (G.E.D.), unless you are a high school graduate already. Most high schools offer G.E.D. programs, and books on taking the G.E.D tests can be found at all public libraries. Most G.E.D. programs are inexpensive or, sometimes, offered free. Call your local school district office to learn what options you have. You will probably have many.

Second, do not think that you must wait four, five, or more years, until you have a college degree. You can enroll in your chosen program of studies spend six months making good progress and attendance records, then present this evidence to a potential employer to show that you are steadily working toward bettering yourself. This often works nicely.

Some years ago, I counseled a man of forty-three who had a highly responsible position with an American importer-exporter. On a trip to Macao, he had been offered a much more responsible job with another American firm, with tremendous salary and benefits, such as unrestricted air travel worldwide. Oddly, he was hesitant about taking the job. He had never completed his college courses and had been hired by the original company in a lower-echelon position. He had used his natural aptitude and ability to rise to this higher level. He was actually terrified that the new company would discover he had no college diploma and refuse to hire him.

I was aware that there was a way out for him because of new college programs that allow students to work on their own time and not attend classes. These are only for already employed persons who wish to specialize. After I explained this to the man, he did locate this program and enrolled. Fortunately, his new employer did not ask him for proof of education, but I am certain that had the employer done so, his enrollment in this executive program would have impressed them sufficiently. He got the job!

If your ring finger is bent to the middle finger and you are in a similar position, it is time to check your options and get into action before another day has passed. Many fine colleges and universities now offer these part-time attendance, weekend, or night opportunities for adult students. You only need to pick up the telephone to know exactly what you can do.

A policeman I know well and have worked with wished to go farther. He spent three years taking extension courses, some of which were offered on PBS television, and in a short time he had an associates degree in criminal justice, at which time he signed up to complete work for a second degree. He is among the few old-line police officers who have several college degrees.

It is so simple to do this that you will not believe how easy it actually can be. Financial assistance is there, just waiting for you to ask. There may be grants in addition to student loans available at ridiculously low interest rates and long-term financing.

Take that step. You'll never regret it.

RING FINGER BENT TO LITTLE FINGER

This is often seen when the individual's desires and wishes have been stifled for a long time, and he or she has lost the ability to analyze what is wrong.

However this happens, if the ring finger is curved toward the little finger, you are the victim of some kind of deprivation. Although it is rare for an individual to deprive him or herself of freedom of action, it does happen. In some cases, it is because as the oldest child in a family you took on responsibilities for younger siblings. In other cases, it is your parents you had to care for. But however it happened, your creativity and self-identification have been submerged and shut off.

You need to go on with your own life as soon as possible. Probably you are not now responsible for younger children, but perhaps you are still taking care of one or more parents. There is assistance available for you in this circumstance, and you must take advantage of it before it is too late and your entire life has been spent in servitude.

First check what assistance is possible, and then follow the exact same steps outlined above for the ring finger bending to the middle finger, *after* you have determined in just which direction you would have gone if you had been free to do so.

In addition, you might use some symbols of your new independence. Buy some new, flattering clothing. Spend two nights a week doing aerobics or some challenging exercise. Have your hair styled, colored, and cut. Get new, flattering eyeglasses. Have a manicure. If you are a woman, have a color and makeup analysis done, no matter what your age. If you are a man, have a color analysis done, and see a tailor about fitting your new clothing so that it will fit *only you*. Buy a signet ring or an I.D. bracelet with your name on it. Visit a line-dancing class or something similar. In other words, try as hard as you can to make yourself look and feel new and different as well as distinctive. These psychological boosts are symbols, but they will help you change the way you look at yourself. They will assert your independence from "yesterday's you."

After you have done this, it will be easier to follow through with the educational steps you'll be planning next.

You might not need any college to achieve independence, but a specialized course might be just the thing. Hundreds of these are available in adult education programs offered at larger schools in your area. Just call and check. They'll give you all of the advice you need.

BENT LITTLE FINGER

It is not unusual to see a bent little finger on a hand, especially an emotional or mental hand.

You must first eliminate the bending that occurs when the lower knuckle, between the bottom and middle finger sections, is slightly bent inward toward the ring finger. This is a health indication, not a psychological indication, although many times a particular personal stress may result in the physical problem. This inward-bent knuckle indicates that there may be prostate trouble for a male individual, or some gynecological problem.

I recently read an entire article devoted to such untruths as "all crooked little fingers belong to liars." We already know that this is ridiculously untrue, as this crooked finger is almost always a health indicator.

The mark of the liar is the little finger bent sideways so that the nail faces away from the rest of the hand. This is possibly a childhood indication that just never straightened out in the adult. A slight twist may belong to the person who merely tends to exaggerate things colorfully, such as saying he or she saw a three-million-pound elephant in the parade. Or the type that listens while you tell a story about some terrible thing that happened to you, and then butts in with a story to top yours. We all know people like this, but it is only in the handprint that it shows up so clearly.

Should you note this finger twist on your own hand, you can make a stronger effort to be certain that you are always telling the truth and not embroidering the facts. If the tendency continues, you might utilize it by writing fiction. Novels are products of a person's imagination, and if you find yourself tempted to tell stories, you might want to take some creative writing courses.

If the little finger bends in a curve with the tip coming in toward the ring finger, then the indication is that your ability to communicate freely has been stifled, or that you've lost touch with your own needs and desires.

Many times we think that we really know what is good for

us, and yet we desire other things about which we are not so certain. Everyone also has unpleasant thoughts at times, and we seem to spend so much of our lives trying to subdue those "demons" in our minds.

If there is a sharply pointed tip on this little finger, you may have a sharp wit. If the finger is bent in, the wit may be aimed at others to make them feel silly or to cut them down. Should you possess wit, you should restrain any urge to use it that way. If you concentrate on using your humor for fun and not as a weapon, you will be respected and considered an excellent conversationalist. Negative wit is really a defense used to cover up one's own shortcomings. It is barbed to hurt. But it has a reverse side as well, and you must find how to use it.

Career for sharp, pointed little fingers:

Writer for commercials	Public speaker
Writer for comedians	Motivational seminars
Novelist	Home shopping channel host

In order to discover if there is a pointed tip, take the finger and place it flat on the paper so that the entire fingertip prints.

If the little finger is just bent inward with the gentle curve toward the ring finger, look closely at the finger sections and measure both sides of each. There should be one segment that measures longer by an eighth of an inch or so on the outside than on the inside. Use the following to interpret what this section indicates.

LOWER SECTION

It is your urges and needs that are being stifled and cut off. Whether someone else is doing this, or you have become so introverted that you no longer see yourself as others see you, you will have to make some changes in this vicious circle, for the longer it continues the more you will lose touch with yourself.

In addition, your personal sexual nature may not be satisfied or maybe repressed for some reason. There are as many possible reasons for this as states in the union, and you will have to make your own determination as to what the cause is.

I suggest that if you cannot find out what it is, or cannot do anything about it yourself, seek help by asking your physician for a referral to a sexual dysfunction clinic if there is no physical problem present.

I have seen this segment on the hand of a person who had been sexually harassed on the job more than once. If that kind of tension exists in your place of work, it is time to move on to another job or seek redress.

Should there also be a deep horizontal block or two across this finger section, it is likely to be related to a sexual problem.

MIDDLE SECTION OF LITTLE FINGER CURVED

This finger section deals with your mathematical ability, as well as your ability to analyze yourself and your actions, whether and under what circumstances you feel guilty about your actions.

This finger represents the ID, our deepest hidden nature and desires. Many of us feel guilty when we have a desire we believe someone else would look down upon. Some are made to feel guilty because they have a big nose, a birthmark, skin of the wrong color, or slanted eyes—all the result of genetics. You should not feel guilty about something you did not choose, but often enough you do. Recently there was a program on television about fat, and specifically fat children. Those little ones were made to feel guilty and undesirable just because their bodies were not of "perfect" shape. And it is only two or three hundred years since it was fashionable to be built like that. Women pinned ruffles inside their bodices to look busty and wire cages on their derrieres to provide a large back end in 1904!

Scientists have recently observed that obesity is not a result of being a pig and eating everything that doesn't eat you first, but a genetic inability to burn up food as most bodies do. It's about time! But it is too late for many who already have a guilt complex.

If this is your problem, stop feeling guilty and go find a doctor who can deal with the problem, whatever it is. Or see a cosmetic counselor who can help you change the look of your nose, your birthmark, your eyes.

If it is something you have done, or fear you have done, then you should ask forgiveness and resolve never to do it again. Then put it out of your mind.

When you begin to feel better about yourself, then you are ready to take steps toward the new you, and a new, more fulfilling career.

TIP SECTION OF LITTLE FINGER CURVED

We have already discussed most of the problems with this finger section if it is twisted away. If it merely leans toward the ring finger, however, then it indicates that you are being stifled in communication somehow. There are several possible reasons for this, including a large, noisy family of extroverts in which you are the only introvert; a bad marriage in which you must be silent and endure; an abusive marriage in which you feel you cannot cry out for help; an abusive father or mother; watching someone else being abused and having to bite your tongue; the feeling that there is no one who cares to listen to you; or just a general feeling of inferiority.

There may also be a blocking horizontal line across this tip, indicating further lack of communication.

Of course, if you can overcome feelings of inferiority and begin to work toward bringing out the real person inside your shell, this will change. Most people who cannot communicate their real feelings and thoughts do develop a shell, like that of a turtle, inside which they dwell, insulating themselves from the cruelty of the world or a specific person.

I do not ordinarily counsel divorce, but if the problem is a cruel or abusive husband, there may be no other choice. Women can seek help and counsel at a shelter, even if they just call and do not actually go there. If you are in this situation, take advantage of whatever type of family counseling you can find, even if you have to go by yourself. (The same advice applies if the problem is an abusive mother or father.)

Never just run away. There are better answers, and you must seek them out. If it is your child or children who are the target of abuse, get help *immediately*.

When you are suffering in one of the situations above, it is hard to find a good job and hard to do good work in any kind of employment.

Gaining peace of mind and protection for the helpless should be your first concern. You must do whatever is necessary to protect them, and yourself. Never assume that abusers will or can change. They will probably never change. But if you are caught in this type of situation, *you* must change—and be a silent doormat no more.

Once you have gotten out of this repressive situation and have any job at all, you can care for yourself, and your children can be aided by one of several agencies while you get on your feet and work toward a satisfying job and eventually a new career.

A career in helping others who have suffered as you have can be the most rewarding and satisfying. For instance

Preschool teacher	School counselor
Social worker	Family and children's service worker
Adoptions agent	Psychologist
Family planning clinic	Child psychologist
Grammar school teacher	Counselor of battered women

I have seen women who have almost reached the emotional snapping point come out of this very successfully and some are even teaching self-defense and martial arts classes to others.

THUMB TWISTS

Normally the thumb shows about three-quarters of its width on a handprint. This is enough to show the basic shape and the type of print it carries.

When the thumb prints narrowly and sideways, then the individual is in some way turning away from himself or herself. If it is continually held with the nail facing away, then the individual expects that the world owes him a living.

If this is the case, the owner may be somewhat disinclined to work toward any goal. He or she may do just enough work to avoid being fired; and if a job is lost, this person is happy just to collect unemployment until a new job falls into his or her lap.

A complete changeover and self-analysis must be made by such a person. It may be difficult to get such a person motivated, but it can be done. It would be surprising for this type of individual to be reading this book, which is geared toward helping you help yourself, but they might pick up a copy.

If so, then all is not lost.

At this point, go back and read over the book once more to find your best field and then set out a short-term and long-term goal structure for yourself.

Anything can be changed, including any aspect of the human personality. This is the basis of such stories as *A Christmas Carol* by Charles Dickens, along with many others. And as long as you are willing to try, you can change.

The bends and twists of the four fingers and thumb upon a hand can offer a complete psychological analysis, even without the actual handprint.

After a radio show I did on CBS back in 1969, prints were sent in to the station to be analyzed. One dear little lady hadn't heard the part about the inked print, and only sat down and drew around her hand. The show's hosts thought that if I was real, I could do an analysis with only this outline. Naturally, I did, and the lady called the program to thank me for saying so many nice things about her, for they were all true.

Never ignore a bending finger. You may be able to avoid a situation before it takes hold.

11

THOSE BUMPS ON THE HAND

Under each finger and around the palmar area are elevated areas. These bumps used to be named for the planets, but in this more enlightened age we can dispense with such an identification system.

Some hands seem to have deep hollows in their centers, with thin pads around the outside. This very deep hollow usually indicates depression in the psychological sense.

Then there are hands that are almost flat, but the basic feeling and texture is still resilient to the touch. If a hand has a soft feeling like a balloon only half filled by air, it is a sign of some health problem, more than likely low blood pressure and poor circulation.

There is another type of hand that has firm, raised pads either all around the middle of the palm, or on at least one side—left, right, top, or bottom of the palm. These highly padded places lend emphasis to those portions of the psychological makeup indicated by their placement on the hand. To view these, hold your hand, palm up, at eye level, and look

The Finger Rulerships

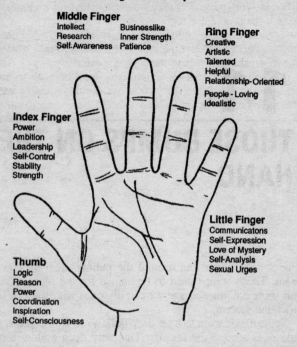

Middle Finger
Intellect   Businesslike
Research   Inner Strength
Self-Awareness   Patience

Ring Finger
Creative
Artistic
Talented
Helpful
Relationship-Oriented

People - Loving
Idealistic

Index Finger
Power
Ambition
Leadership
Self-Control
Stability
Strength

Little Finger
Communicatons
Self-Expression
Love of Mystery
Self-Analysis
Sexual Urges

Thumb
Logic
Reason
Power
Coordination
Inspiration
Self-Consciousness

across it toward the fingertips. You should easily be able to see which portions of the palm are highly padded.

This will also show up clearly on the handprint. Some portions that are not well padded, or almost flat, will not print at all. This is why it is necessary to place a thick and folded towel beneath the paper you are using, to allow the hand to bestow equal pressure in all areas.

If there are white spots still, even with this thick padding beneath your paper, then they have specific meanings and may show problems to be solved in your career analysis.

Any area on the palm or fingers can show a spot where there

is a current problem, going on right now. It may not have been like that yesterday, and may be gone, filled in, a month from now *if* the problem it represents has been corrected.

Look at the map on the facing page. It is similar to one you saw earlier. The areas on it can be affected by these whiteouts, however, showing where the problem exists.

Correspondingly, a very dark area may be seen in any of these areas, similar to the look of the dominant finger we saw much earlier in the book. This is called a pressure point.

Either a complete whiteout or a darkened area on the palm will indicate stress in that area of life.

These areas include:

Motivation	Under index finger
Learning	Middle
Creating	Ring
Communicating	Little
Analyzing	Outside of palm
Feeling	Lower outside palm
Intuitive Response	Center bottom of palm
Experiencing	Base Section of thumb
Reacting	Between thumb and index
Changing	Center of palm

If there is a whiteout on any of these areas, then this is the area in which your present interruption or problem is going on.

A whiteout in the motivation area is common, when you are in a period of making no progress or feeling that you are not moving forward. Boredom may set in, and you might have lost your motivation for a short time. This would probably create a darkening of the area.

A whiteout under the middle finger, in the area of learning, might be seen if something has occurred to stop your process of learning and doing.

A darkening under the ring finger, in creativity, might show that you are suffering from not being able to utilize your natural aptitude to create. A whiteout would indicate the same thing, but it will have gone on for a longer period.

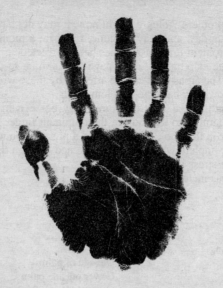

This hand shows both darkened pressure points and shark bites or white-outs, mostly in the area of motivation and self-esteem.

A darkened area under the little finger indicates that there is a problem in being able to communicate and share. A whiteout would show that the problem is short-term.

Either a whiteout or a darkening might appear on the mid-section of your little finger showing that you have a situation you are unable to figure out or analyze. It may not even be your problem, but it might be up to you to solve it. The whiteout would indicate much less long-standing problems.

In the imaginitive area of the hand, a darkening of the area of feeling is not uncommon. It indicates there is some type of blocking influence on your feelings and that you may have had something happen that left you uncertain how to proceed. It may be that you have had your feelings hurt somehow. A whiteout would show that the problem is not long-standing.

At the base of the hand, a whiteout is seen frequently. It often indicates that you have a sort of psychic hunch that you should or should not do something and are holding back because of this. A darkening here indicates a longer-lasting situation.

The area under the thumb is quite frequently darkened when you are undergoing a lot of hectic or stressful events in both business and personal life. In fact, it is possible to have both darkened areas and whiteouts here in combination. When this is seen, it shows that you are busy with a great many things in your life and career and that you are worried about some of them. Many of these may be of great significance, as this portion of the hand is the largest in area and is also the base of a digit.

If this area prints cleanly, with no darkened areas and no whiteouts, then things are going pretty normally, and you are in control.

A whiteout on the flexure line at the base of the thumb's middle section indicates a problem with the family or a family member, or that you were concerned and worried about such a person.

A whiteout of the intensity line indicates that you are worrying about something you have no control over at all; no matter what you do, you cannot affect what is happening.

Similarly, a whiteout in the reacting area between thumb and forefinger indicates that you are reacting to some stimulus, good or bad. You must check the remainder of the hand to determine what this might be.

Whiteouts are common also in the center of the hand and may appear when things are changing and you do not know where things are likely to go next. They can also be seen when you are tired from too much work or traveling constantly to new places on business, with little time to rest.

Look at the handprint of Lady Sarah Churchill, daughter of the late great Winston Churchill. In the U.S. for a trip to promote a book about her father (which she had not written.) Lady Churchill was absolutely exhausted, but very graciously allowed me to black her hand and take her print in the green

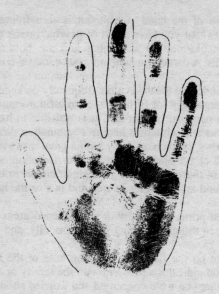

room after we were on the same television show. Her lady-in-waiting was appalled and tried to drag her away, but she insisted on staying and making the print.

You can see that the thumb itself did not print clearly, nor did the index. There is a whiteout in the "experience" area; in the center of the palm there are several big whiteouts; and the middle of both middle and ring fingers did not print. Darkening appears under the middle, ring, and little fingers, as well as on the tip of the middle and ring fingers.

All of this echoes her exhaustion, that she was on an errand not her own, and that there was a good deal of pressure on her motivation, her emotional balance, her organization, and her idealistic nature. The darkened tip on the little finger is on communications; it appears because she was engaged in trying to acquaint the United States with what her father had stood for and accomplished.

The darkening under the middle, ring, and little fingers tells us that she was trying to learn, create an effect, and communicate something special to our country.

All of these viewpoints would, of course, be critical to one with an emotional mental hand. Getting the point across clearly would be her only goal.

The hand is unusual in that this type of hand, the emotional, hardly ever has such a massively dominant index finger. This unusual dominance is echoed by the clear, commanding signature. All in all a remarkable woman, under stress, worn out but ever gracious.

Her career direction would be in some area of art, and in working toward environmental balance. She is an idealist, but with that dominant index, an intensely practical realist at the same time. Her prints contain arches and loops. She is a natural diplomat.

"SHARK BITES"

When a print is made, sometimes there are whiteouts on the fingers as well as the palm. They are likely to appear anywhere around all four sides of any finger section, left or right, tip or bottom. Darkening spots are much more likely to cover the entire finger section, as they are a palmar section.

We call the whiteouts "shark bites" as they look just as if a small shark had come up and bitten your finger, taking out a small, irregular area that remains white.

The shark bites on your own hands may be significant indicators in your career analysis. Here's what they mean:

Tip of index finger	1. Problem in what you do to express yourself
Tip of middle finger	1. Problem in your career 2. Problem in being organized 3. Fear of failure

Tip of ring finger	1. Problems with other people

Tip of little finger	1. Problems with being able to communicate
	2. Not being able to determine where you are going

Thumb	1. Loss of control of your life
	2. Being unfulfilled
	3. Being unsatisfied with your progress

Shark bites may appear on any finger section. If they are near the bottom of the section, the problem is new and is in operation at the present moment. Near the center of the section, a shark bite indicates a problem of two to three months' age. At the top of any finger section, the indication is that the problem has been in force for six months or more and may have been fully or partially resolved.

Small, seemingly insignificant problems may cause these whiteouts on the hand if they are a threat to your personal well-being and psychological balance.

An unbalanced life that is out of control will show a great many of these whiteouts either on the palm or on both the palm and the fingers.

These indications cannot be seen on a bare hand. This is why it is important to take a good, clear, inked handprint, and to follow up this original self-analysis with prints taken at either three- or six-month intervals.

A continual whiteout in any specific area of the fingers or palm will show that the problem is not only long lasting, but is still in effect. Only a solution will remove this "erasing" of the skin patterns from the hand.

In Dallas, Texas, some twenty years ago I was challenged by a student who was a physicist. He insisted that these darker or whiteout areas were an accident and would change depending on how you made your print or how much pressure you put on the hand while making the print.

Areas Affected by Whiteouts or Pressure Points

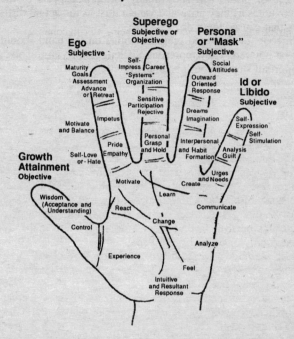

Accepting the challenge, I asked him to spend part of the upcoming lunch break in making more prints of his hand. I instructed him to take one against the wall, on the floor with another student pressing down on his hand, on a countertop—wherever he wanted and any way he could think of to print one.

At the end of the lunch break I returned to find a student with a shamefaced, puzzled look, staring at twelve prints of his hand, all taken differently and all showing the exact same shark bites and pressure points as had the first.

Naturally I accepted his apology.

You can watch these areas of pressure as they move up each finger section as the problem disappears or is solved. A complete file of prints will show many different aspects of the problem areas as they arise and vanish; just as the actual difficulties that caused them do.

Whiteouts or darkened pressure points on the hand should never be ignored. They represent challenges for you to solve, an important step in your personal growth.

12

AT YOUR FINGERTIPS

Your fingernails may reveal some important things about you and how you approach life in general, as well as some hints toward career directions.

Fingernails usually take six months to completely grow out, except for the thumb, which may take nine. Their curvature, from side to side, forming an irregular arch, or from tip to base, will reveal possible problems with posture and the condition of the spine. White spots do not indicate fate, fame, or fortune. They may represent calcium deposits, or just a slight injury to the nail. These appear and disappear constantly.

Fingernail shape, however, is determined in the first year of life, and is generally the same throughout life.

Basic shaping of the nails may differ from finger to finger, but usually only slightly. Thumbs may be broader in appearance than other nails, and the nail on a little finger may be smaller or narrower than others.

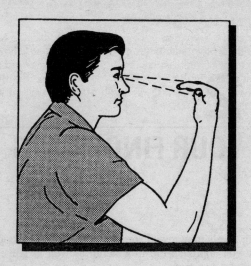

How to look at fingernail arches

NAIL SHAPES

Nails are categorized into seven basic shapes and styles, each with its own meaning.

The names of these types are old-fashioned, but they do tell us something about how the personality is based, and what career tips can be gained from a given shape.

The very best way to observe your fingernails is by bending the fingers and pointing them toward you at eye level. In this way the general shape of all four nails will be revealed clearly.

As you identify them, you can make a notation on one of the practice blanks in this book. Remember that if you are printing a friend or family member, the nail shapes will not be shown on the inked print, so you must examine each of them and make a note of its shape on the print.

"PSYCHIC": THIN, HIGH-ARCHED, PINK-COLORED NAILS

This identification does not mean you should be able to take on Wall Street experts at their own game, but it does show that you tend to gain impressions about people, places, and situations "out of thin air" so to speak. You will work rapidly and intuitively at any given task, and will often be finished with a job long before anyone else would be done.

Careers: Any job that allows you some freedom of choice, without a rigid time schedule; any job that does not tie you to a desk during the entire work period; and careers where learn-

Seven Basic Types of Fingernail

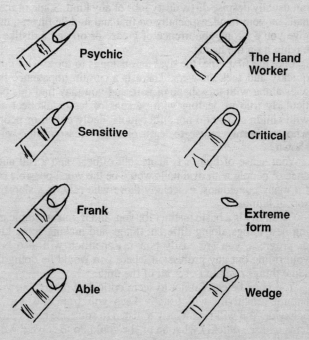

Psychic

The Hand Worker

Sensitive

Critical

Frank

Extreme form

Able

Wedge

ing, evaluating, and assessing are essential components. Avoid any job that is constricting or does not allow you any freedom of movement or some flexibility of hours.

These nails have the highest arches of all the types and are a longish oval. They usually are rose pink in color with large moons.

KEY WORD: PARTICULAR

SENSITIVE: OVAL, ARCHED, LIGHT PINK NAILS

The sensitive nail is closely akin to the psychic shape, and belongs to persons who may enjoy gardening or plant culture, but usually despise dirty, dusty jobs of any kind. Some of these nails on your hand, especially on first and middle fingers, may give you a strong abhorrence of grease or oil and a dislike of having it on the hands.

Like the first type, the oval nail belongs to those who think quickly and seek answers. There is a certain impatience that goes along with this shape of nail, and you may find this particularly true in dealing with persons of lesser intellect and with children. You do not suffer fools gladly either, or people who stubbornly refuse to learn or to see reason after being shown.

Your sense of humor is acute, but offbeat, and a full audience of people with oval nails would be the worst possible one for many comedians, especially those who rely on a slapstick sort of humor.

Creativity is a basic instinct for you, and if you are not learning new things, doing different things and making some kind of progress, you are easily bored. Repetition will also bore you, ruling out any profession where you would be doing the same things over and over all of the time.

You must be careful not to seem critical of others, but your natural sensitivity will usually keep you from this sort of behavior. You will find it easy to listen to someone else's problems and see quickly what he or she could do to solve the difficulties. Because you do not like to take advice from others, you may become somewhat impatient when the one you are advising refuses to listen or take action.

Boredom, illness, too much repetition, and lack of progress are all downfalls for you, and if you are in such a situation with no hope for change, your health and energy will be affected. Depression could be the result, if you are not careful to find some hobby or pastime that supplies the stimulation you require.

Career Choices:

Supervisory work

Business administration

Designing of any sort

Field sales

Botanical or horticultural work

Writing

Cinematography

Environmental research

Filming documentaries

Television and media
    researcher

Executive secretary

Tour guide

Psychologist

These nails are usually rounded ovals, light to medium pink in color, with large, white moons. If the nail is very pale, there may be a mineral deficiency, and either an additive should be taken, or a diet rich in minerals should be followed.

KEY WORD: RESPONSIVE

FRANK: ROUNDED, PINK, MEDIUM MOONS

This nail is the most commonly found as shapes go. It is slightly arched, oval in outline, and may take up half of the fingertip's space. The owner of this nail is often a good advice-giver, as he or she will usually tell you the truth, the whole truth, and nothing but the truth, as the saying goes.

Sometimes, however, this frankness may get the owner into trouble. If you have this nail, you will no doubt already be aware of the fact that you must learn to be more diplomatic with others, and to overlook some things rather than criticize. It is also a good idea to wait to give an opinion until you've been asked for one. Then take a minute to think before you give it. The minute is important, for if you speak without thinking you may find yourself hurting rather than helping.

Once you have learned these things, you make not only a fine friend, but also a good boss, because careful self-control and policing of your tendency to be too blunt can result in an open, accepting personality.

Naturally, if there is only one frank nail on the hand, this will be only a latent tendency and will not prove to be a problem. If all or most of the nails are this type, you will have to be extra considerate and careful.

Creative and talented, an individual with this arched fingernail has quick perception and many abilities.

Careers:

Antiques or gift shop owner	Talk show host
Clothing and fashion industry	Nurse or Technician
Computer operation	Media
Real estate sales and brokering	Military
Fashions or clothing	Mailroom or post office
Cosmetician	Government
Sales	Police dispatcher
Reporter or journalist	

This nail is seen to have a low arch, and is given to splitting (top layer coming loose). Color is medium pink, with wide moons. Often this fingernail will seemingly never grow past the tip of the finger, and may break or crack off upon impact with a door or wall.

KEY WORD: HASTY

ABLE: LOW ARCH, PINK, SMALLER MOON

This nail has an extremely low arch, or is almost flat on the fingertip.

It belongs to the person who can do almost anything well, and has more than one talent. Usually flexible, adaptable, and well balanced, if you have this nail on four or more of your fingers, you may have had some trouble figuring out what career direction to take, as you had so many interests.

If you have spent part of your life in one career, it had some attraction for you that kept your interest. It is unusual, however, for people with this nail to stay at one single career throughout life.

Your fast-changing interests may encourage you to take up one or more hobbies, which might become so very attractive that you will one day quit working to spend all of your time at one of them. In that case, the hobby could become your job.

You have a basic restlessness of mind which will lead you to explore many different ideas until you find the one that is just right for you.

You will usually learn faster and more completely when you can watch someone doing something, and your visual perception is good. You may find it more difficult to learn something from reading it than from seeing it done. Sheets of printed instructions will frustrate you, yet you are adept at solving problems and puzzles that require hand-eye coordination and basic intelligence.

You will enjoy showing others how to do something, and in many ways would be happy as a teacher as long as the subject you were teaching offered some variety.

Because you do not have a large ego, you find it easy to work with others and to understand other points of view. You may have a genius for figuring out what makes others tick and for motivating them. You are especially good with children and young people.

Challenges are vital to you, and you will often excel in some type of physical activity or sport. You will find relief from a boring job with aerobics, a cross-country skiing machine, or just walking outdoors, which you love and appreciate.

Career choices:

Teaching	Oceanographer
Adult intruction	Science
Crafts, mechanical	Physics

Law enforcement
Group leader
Politics
Law
Textbook author
Personal trainer
Naturalist, forest ranger

Medicine
Physical therapist
Emergency medicine
Jeweler or silversmith
Couturier or tailor
Outdoor sports

If the nail is almost flat and a light to deep pink color, with a wider, flattish moon, it is of the able type. Even one nail of this type on each hand adds variety to the psyche. The nail often does not grow past the fingertip, which can be frustrating to many women. Increased calcium and iron in the diet may help. The fingernail's moon is often almost the same color as the rest of the nail, and if so, there may be poor circulation in the hands and feet. Regular exercise should remedy this problem.

Almost 50 percent of all nails are of this type, especially on male hands.

KEY WORD: ABILITY

THE HAND WORKER: TAN OR DARKER PINK, SMALL MOON

Quite flat in appearance, this fingernail marks the person who may work with his or her mind, but needs something to do with the hands as well. Many individuals with this nail in executive-level jobs will have a home woodworking shop or some absorbing hobby that involves the use of the hands. A fine balance of work styles must be achieved for a person with this nail to really enjoy life.

If the job itself requires some amount of dexterity, then satisfaction will be much easier to reach.

The person's intelligence is quite high, and the creativity level can be even higher. Unlike the older thinking about large, strong hands with massive fingers and flat nails, they do not belong to people of a primitive type—as stated in obsolete books on palm reading and disproved by hand analysts—but to the specialist! In putting this type of nail to work, some area of intricate and demanding specialization is required as well as natural dexterity.

"People skills" are good in this personality, and if you have this type of nail you possess the ability to work well as part of a group with a similar goal. Giving by nature, you will do well at any job that involves service or the betterment of others.

Those who have this nail often sacrifice their own needs and wants to help or assist others.

Careers:

Medical specialization	Sports coach
Surgery	Youth counselor
Emergency medicine	Psychologist
911 operator	Hypnotherapist
Ambulance attendant or EMT	School nurse, counselor
Watchmaker or jeweler	Plastics industry
Cabinetmaker	Biochemistry
Interior rehabilitation	Bioengineering
Land developer	Civil engineering
Architect	Pilot
Commercial artist	Airline attendant
Teacher	Sculptor

This flat, tan-colored or pink nail is often found on a thumb, adding the ability to specialize to any set of job skills. While the able nail works in creating a jack of all trades, the hand-worker nail pushes one to develop his or her area of specialization. I have seen this nail on the hands of plastic surgeons, a professor of physics, and a woman who grew award-winning roses.

It is an all-round talent indicator, but if pushed into a routine job, the owner will stifle without something to do with the hands.

If the nail is tan-colored and the moon is almost invisible, there may be some mineral deficiency or a tendency to breathe too shallowly. Deep breathing exercises, aerobic exercise, and a vitamin-rich diet will help.

KEY WORD: SPECIALIST

CRITICAL: PALE, FLAT OR DISHED

This nail is not often seen on all of the fingers. It is more common on the little finger, along with a pointed tip. If it is on one or more of your fingers, you must use care not to be too critical of others' actions or personalities. You may have a tendency to be similarly critical of yourself, especially if the middle section of the little finger is the largest on that finger, or is crossed by many horizontal lines.

With one or more of these nails, however, you have a unique ability to spot flaws in any subject or object. As a troubleshooter you have no peer, for these tiny flaws that might seem insignificant to others will stand out as warning flags to you.

If you control this tendency to be judgmental, then you can be the warmest and most considerate of friends, and an efficient supervisor or manager as well.

This nail never seems to get anywhere near the end of the fingertip, and may be slightly dished in, as if it would hold a drop of water on its surface. It can be caused by a very abusive childhood or troubled adolescence.

Career choices:

Fiction writer	Corrections officer
Media work	Social work
Professional illustrator	Politics
Artist	Contractor
Museum curator	Handyman
Window dresser	Gardener, botanist
Appliance sales	Veterinarian
Aerospace industry	Zoo technician
Real estate	Animal breeding, showing
Drug enforcement	

This nail may be round or squared in shape, with almost no moon at all. It may be the result of an injury to that fingertip at some past time, but if there is more than one on the hand, or one on the same finger of opposite hands, it is likely to be a natural fingernail shape.

It is most commonly found on the little finger, but may be seen on the ring finger on some hands. If you do have this nail, you will find that you are able to learn your job so well that you can work without supervision for days at a time.

This critical nail may be medium pink to dark pink in color, or may have a brownish tinge. It is brittle and may break at the tip, making it even shorter. It should always be filed to a squared tip to minimize damage.

KEY WORD: LONER

WEDGE: PALE, FLAT, TINY BASE

This nail was once thought to belong to people with some unusual circulatory problem. It is found on the hands of persons who have little patience with their fellow man (or woman) and who require a large amount of physical activity in their work.

There may be a problem with temper, although usually a person who has these nails will have learned to control this aspect by late adolescence.

If this tendency is controlled, there is almost an explosive enthusiasm and energy connected with having this nail. Such vital and distinctive emotions need an outlet, and this is usually a physical one.

If you have this nail, you might try challenging yourself in other than physical ways. Games that require strategy or hobbies that require concentration might be a fine outlet for your excess energy.

Once the tendency toward a quick temper is tamed, you can be the finest of workers toward any given goal.

Careers:

Fireman	Tour guide
Paramedic	Photographer

Key to Bitten Fingernails

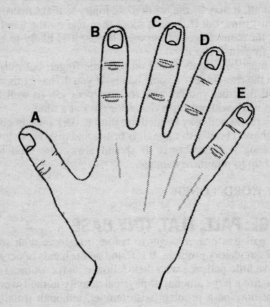

Sports	Magazine or newspaper
Physical therapist	columnist
Sports medicine	Restaurant work
Environmentalist	Short-order cook
Recycling expert	Dietitian

This nail can be a problem for manicurists, since the tip often overlaps the flesh of the fingertip and forms a little hook. The moon may be very small if the wedging is extreme.

This is a most unusual nail.

KEY WORD: ENERGY

Not all hands will have the same basic type of fingernail on all five digits. Usually there will be only two types, and one of the different ones may be found on either thumb or little finger. It is possible to have unusual fingernails appearing anywhere on the hand, however, and if it is not an accidental shape due to a blow or injury, then it should be read as described in the section above.

If your hand does have all the same nails on fingers and thumb, you are part of the largest group of humans, for, while the fingerprints can be and usually are very different from one another on any hand, the nails show much more uniformity.

Toenails have a great deal in common with fingernails, and if there is a residual effect from a whiplash, for instance, both the thumbnail and the nail on the large toe will be similarly shaped, often causing a hangnail on the thumb and an ingrown nail on the toe.

Bends in the fingers, their prints, and even the nails do have a great deal to tell you about your vocational aptitudes and directions.

BITTEN NAILS

According to most medical authorities, biting the nails is an indication of stress, lack of self-esteem, and even of fear of one type or another.

In hand analysis, we know that the bitten fingernail is a symptom of some problem in life. Many of these problems involve the profession or the workplace.

A. THUMB

If you have a habit of biting your thumbnail, on the top or on either side, there is something you know you should be doing and you are avoiding doing it.

Since thumbs indicate motivation, willpower, and the reasoning faculty, constant biting of the nail indicates that there is a problem in these areas.

For instance, you might be unhappy at your job and know that you should take some action; yet you decide to wait. In another instance, you may have been offered the opportunity to take some training that would lead to a better job or a promotion where you are already working; yet you have been stalling.

A nagging feeling that you should be doing *something* and for whatever reason are not following through may cause you to bite your thumbnail.

B. INDEX

Biting this fingernail often indicates that you are having second thoughts about whatever you are doing. It can also indicate that you are working at a job that is much less challenging than you prefer.

If you have a habit of biting the index fingernail, you may be ashamed of or worried about something you have done. Since it is the finger of ego, the way in which we see ourselves, biting this nail will usually indicate that your feelings about yourself are unresolved or negative.

C. MIDDLE

If the middle fingernail is the one you usually bite, then your conscience may be bothering you. This indication can also be found when your entire life and your career are in a disorganized state.

Since this finger stands for your true inner self, the habit of biting the nail indicates that there is a problem in either your direction or your progress.

If you are forcing yourself to keep working at a job you dislike or actually hate, the rest of your life will also be in disorder, and you may bite this nail.

D. RING

When the ring fingernail is the one being chewed or bitten, then your problem is not with you, but with other people. It

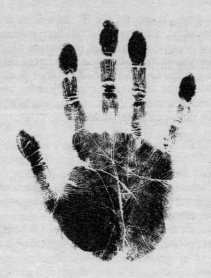

This female has bitten fingernails on index and ring fingers. Note the blocks and whiteouts on both.

might be that you are experiencing problems with a boss or supervisor.

This nail is on the finger that stands for the personality you create to show the world, and any problem with this self-image will be reflected in the rest of the life. This fingernail may be an indication of trouble in your personal, family, or romantic life as well.

Whether the problem is with you and your image, or with people in your life, this is an indication that you may need some counseling to assist in solving it.

E. LITTLE

My experience shows that this fingernail is not being bitten as often as others, but if it is, there are unresolved desires in your mind that are not being realized.

Since this finger stands for the ID, as well as self-analysis and communication, a bitten fingernail here indicates a problem that must be solved. If you are not certain which area the problem is in, you should take some time to consider whether you are being fulfilled and satisfied by your work and relationships. Do a little self-analysis and discover whether you can locate the problem area that is causing you to bite this nail. This could be time well spent, indeed.

If all of the nails are being bitten, there is a general unhappiness and frustration with all areas of your life. Make an effort to change your surroundings, your career position, or even the people with whom you interact as rapidly as you can.

Nailbiting can be symptomatic of frustration, anger, or rage and should be considered a serious problem.

If the finger flesh on both sides of the nail is being bitten as well, then the problem indicated by that fingernail is even more pressing.

HANGNAILS

Biting the loose bits of skin on the lower side of the nail which we call a hangnail is a reflection of problems with your posture or your spinal column, as discussed in my first book. If you are always biting a hangnail, perhaps you should schedule an appointment with a chiropractor or osteopathic physician to locate the problem.

Fingernails can be one of the most interesting aspects of any hand. They have a great deal to tell us about the inner and outer personality, as well as the career or profession best suited to a person.

Remember that the nails cannot be seen on a print, so careful observation should be made and noted on either a practice sheet or an inked handprint.

13

A THUMB IN EVERY PIE

The length, formation, and attitude of the thumb form one of the little extras in hand analysis, for they can be quite instructive.

In past chapters, we have seen that the thumb can be offset, to indicate sports prowess and a sense of rhythm, and that its relative shape and size can tell whether you operate on logic and reason, or just trust your positive feelings and willpower.

The attitude and padding of the thumb can be of great interest as well, for this can tell something about your basic energy quotient. Vocationally, if you have a flaccid thumb, you will definitely not do well in a dynamic job that requires swift action and motion or international travel.

The pad on the thumb tip can be either flattish and soft when it is pressed, almost squishing out of shape; or it can be moderately firm to the touch, springing back when it is pressed down. This would indicate a lessened vitality if soft or normal vitality if spring.

If the thumb pad is almost hard to the touch when it is pressed, then there may be an excess of vitality, and this would suit you for a job that could lead you on a straight track to the top. This dynamic thumb tip indicates a personality ready for jobs requiring independence, quick action, and decision making.

A distinctive type of thumb looks somewhat like a paddle in that the tip section is much broader than the second. This was at one time considered a murderer's thumb by some early palmists, but not much proof exists to support such a label. Persons inclined to that particular type of violence may be found to have one of two fingerprints on the thumb, but the shape of the thumb has nothing to do with this.

A paddle thumb is the mark of a person with great physical strength, as well as an individualized sense of touch and shape. Many sculptors, ceramics experts, and workers in clay have this thumb, which seems almost to be made for working some material into shape. Carpenters and woodworkers may also have such a thumb, as may gardeners.

A small, thin thumb will indicate that ambition and vitality are deficient in some way. A careful analysis of the rest of the hand is necessary to determine just what blocks appear on the fingers, or what other problems there might be. Pay close attention to the bending of the fingers, which may indicate where the basic problem lies.

Individuals with this thumb may be more comfortable in a job that allows them freedom to do competent work but does not force them to make decisions on a day-to-day basis. If the thumb is also closely held to the fingers, a position that does not involve a lot of public contact might be best.

A strong and powerful thumb might reach more than halfway up the lower section of the index finger. This is an excellent indication of a personality that responds well to almost any type of employment in which responsibility is a requirement.

This long thumb will also demand more freedom of action and movement than will a smaller thumb, so career decisions should be made with this demand in mind.

It has been said that the thumb, which is the mark of the sentient being and toolmaker, rules the hand. If the thumb is strong and well shaped, the personality may be stronger and better able to overcome problems indicated on the remainder of the hand.

In my opinion, the thumb is a self-starter portion of the personality, showing how you will face and solve problem situations and difficulties in any area of life.

INWARD BEND

Looking at the thumb, note carefully whether it is essentially straight or whether there is a bend of the tip section in either an inward or outward direction.

If the tip section is bent toward the fingers, then the indication is that you are likely to depend on your inner resources for answers. You prefer small groups of compatible people and may be uncomfortable in a crowd or with a great many strangers.

A job choice should be made to insulate you from large numbers of people.

OUTWARD BEND

An outward bend of the thumb's tip will indicate that you tend to fill your life with friends and are comfortable in a large group.

This is one of the most likely indications of the person who can offer advice and help to others before taking any notice of his or her own needs. This person may actually be teaching others how to handle life's problems and to grow inwardly or even spiritually. If you have this thumb, you may have many close friends and prefer to spend your time with them, even more than you do with your family. You may end up being an instructor or teacher in some context, perhaps helping adults to develop their motivational abilities, or to learn some skill that will better equip them to solve life's problems.

Many individuals with this thumb will spend all or part of

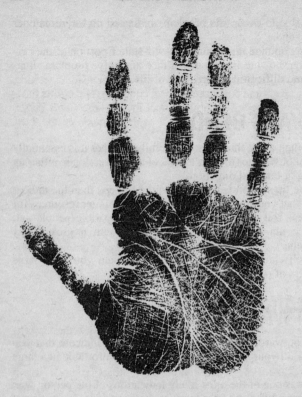

their lives helping humanity as a whole, perhaps in relation to
the environment or global peace.

Look at the hand of Claes Nobel, nephew of the famed originator of the Nobel Prizes. The hand is that of a leader whose
index finger is dominant in delineation and topped with the
loop-arch fingerprint of curiosity and seeking. The major lines
are clear, and creativity is evident in the area under the ring finger. He has the "wild goose" syndrome evident near the base
of the lifeline, indicating some foreign travel and involvement.

His thumb is quite long, very strong, and well separated

from his straight fingers. The *tip* section is slightly bent outward.

Note also the long tips on ring and little fingers, the mark of the teacher.

Nobel is involved in a project of global dimensions, seeking to bring peace and cooperation to all countries. His efforts have resulted in a second group of Nobel Prizes—the Earth Prizes begun in 1991—and this effort involves many of the best thinkers in the world today.

The hand is noteworthy for its clarity and lack of major problems. At the time this print was taken, more than fifteen years ago, Nobel was struggling to put this world coalition together, which accounts for the "shark bites" on fingers and palm. These problems have all been solved, so the hand would look even less blotched if the print were taken today.

The strong, clear thumb on any hand may help to maintain emotional balance, and to assist the person in solving problems.

STRAIGHT THUMB

As we have seen on the hand of Claes Nobel, the straight thumb acts as a balancing factor, as well as a strengthening influence over the remainder of the hand.

Some hands with major pressure points (darkened areas) and shark bites blotting out portions of the fingers and palm have a strong, straight thumb, thus indicating that whatever the problems in personal life or career, these blocks to progress will be eventually cleared away and overcome.

Note the hand of Carl Jung, the great psychologist. The thumb is small and crossed with lines of frustration, but it is straight and at a positive angle to the hand. A short index finger indicates that this individual was best placed in a job that involved research and exploration within a laboratory, rather than a position of leadership.

Strong creativity is shown under the ring finger, and the medical stigmata of upright lines is very large between ring

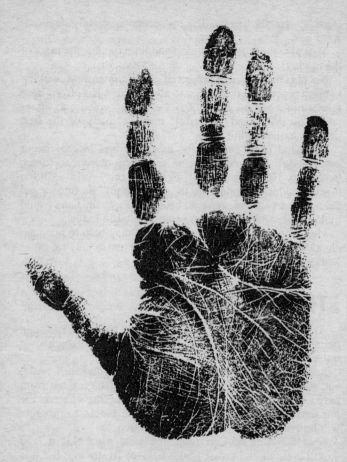

Carl Jung

and little fingers. His interests were obviously in the area of creative medicine. Effort lines are visible on all lower finger sections, broader on the middle sections, and reach the tips of the fingers or organization (middle), teaching (ring), and communication (little), showing that he not only had good ideas, but also was able to communicate them. His books on important aspects of human psychology and personality went far to clarify the earlier ideas of Freud and other pioneer researchers in the human mind.

The hand is of the emotional type, yet is strengthened by the straight, unwavering little finger and the outward bend of the thumb at its tip.

The index fingerprint is the arch, the mark of curious minds, and there is a most unusual print on the ring finger, a small rounded whorl within an arch. This indicates some genius for working with others, and as we know, this is how Jung spent his life.

The hand is covered with extras and clusters of lines, which is common to a hand of this type. It is rare to find a male hand that is so true to the emotional type. This handprint has been reduced in size, and would be much less compressed-looking if shown at its full size.

It is of the "busy" type among emotional hands. It is remarkably free of blocks on any finger sections, except for the middle of the index finger, which might be the result of losing a beloved parent at a fairly young age.

It is an interesting and complex hand, with a smaller but effectively strong thumb.

Another striking hand is that of the *Guinness Book of World Records* star Vernon Craig, whose stage name is Komar, and whose life-style statue adorns the portals of the various Guinness museums nationwide.

Craig's hand shows the strong thumb with a wide-angled position, indicating clearly his strong personality. The middle finger is visibly the dominant one on the hand, indicating a great deal of inner strength as well, in addition to a deep sense of self-control.

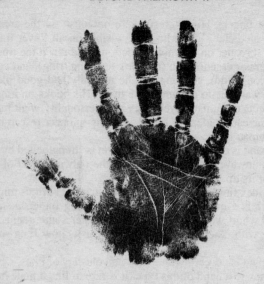

The hand of Vernon Craig "Komar"

The word "strength" applies extremely well in more ways than one to Mr. Craig, as his world records are for amazing feats of strength and daring. Among these are records for the longest, hottest firewalk in history, and for supporting the weight of an entire automobile, upon his prone body—well over a ton of metal, glass, and rubber—while lying on a bed of sharp six-inch nails!

In his professional life, he is an expert cheesemaker and manages a retail store specializing in delicate cheeses made by hand. This business ability is clearly indicated by the long, clear, and well-formed middle finger, his short, tight head line, and the elongated lower sections on both index and middle fingers.

His unusual hobby is an integral portion of life for Craig, who exhibits tremendous concentration and physical strength as he performs his stage act as Komar, the Hindu Fakir.

The act began as an effort to show how much a trained body and mind could accomplish, as a means to raise money for children with disabling handicaps.

His demonstration of bending an iron bar with his bare hands met with resounding success, and he has expanded it into a program seen in many countries around the world as well as on international television.

He is actually a self-described American farm boy and has no Hindu or other Indian blood. Komar, in an effort to help others to learn some part of what he can do, including his amazing ability to almost instantaneously heal injuries to his own body and to stop his blood at will, has written a book, *Life Without Pain*, a Berkley publication.

During the past twenty-five years he has appeared on lecture platforms and demonstrated some of his amazing abilities at conferences devoted to mind and body control.

Cooperating with scientific research teams in laboratories from the U.S. to mainland China is also a part of his constant effort to learn more about how he is able to do some of these things.

His attempt to explain some part of what he is able to do and to teach what he understands of his abilities to others is highlighted by the very long tip on his ring finger, and a correspondingly elongated and developed tip on his little finger. There is a consequent development of the ulnar portion of the hand, although the radial side shows dominance.

A major shark bite has left the tip of the middle finger invisible on this print, and most probably appeared due to conflicts at the time it was taken, between resuming his work at the cheese shop or becoming a full-time performer. The strength of the thumb and the clarity of the skin patterns are quite evident, and would inevitably result in his making the more practical career choice. This is not the hand of a person who would take a risk of that type, although his performing career involves physical risks of all types.

The high-set little finger tells us that he could not leave the spotlight forever, however, and so he has learned to exist in a life that is simultaneously practical *and* utterly romantic and impractical.

Again, the strong and outwardly bent thumb tip reveals his work with the public and his indication to teach others how to better themselves, even if his method could be considered highly unusual.

Note the teacher's square beneath the index finger, creativity beneath the ring finger, and connecting lines between the head and the life line, indicating Craig's complete control over his own mind and ability.

Although the careers of both Carl Jung and Vernon Craig dealt with the mysteries of the human mind, the only connecting link between their two hands is the attitude and bend of their thumbs.

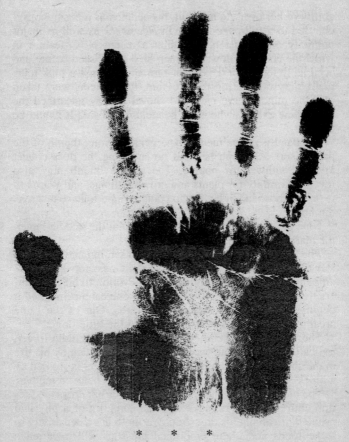

*   *   *

A less physically demanding but interesting life is led by famed Dowser Ron Warmoth.

As a child, he showed unusual psychic abilities because he could read the contents of sealed envelopes without opening them. He also made accurate comments and predictions about the personal lives of complete strangers; and was encouraged and taught by his mother, although she seemingly had no such

ability of her own. As an adult, his acumen as a business psychic led to a full-page feature in *Newsweek* as well as major
publicity on television, including a recent NBC feature in
which he correctly dowsed a map he'd never seen before and
accurately located a deposit of rare and expensive pink tourmaline crystal. During the program, the cameras were taken
into the mine, where pick and shovel rapidly unearthed the
tourmaline exactly where his pendulum had said it would be
found!

His hand is of the mental type, with a strong thumb of the
paddle sort. Although he does no sculpting, he does collect
lovely Southwestern pottery. The paddle thumb may also
reveal an affinity for plants and growing things, and Warmoth
is one of those individuals who could be said to have a "green
thumb."

Note the deep heart line ending almost at the middle finger,
the mark of the "giver."

The little finger is dominant and high set, indicating that he
is well suited to a profession that demands not only some
amount of public speaking, but also devotion to helping others to better themselves. There is only one career line, and it
begins slightly in the subconscious area. Out of the same
area, psychic lines flare upward toward the little finger.

There is a slight bending of the tip on the middle finger,
indicating that in some ways Warmoth does not enjoy his life
in the spotlight. The middle section of this finger is crossed by
a block, which is the result of the loss of his beloved mother.

The blocking line on the little finger does not cross the section entirely, thus putting it into the category of a physical
problem involving his digestion. Warmoth has a sensitivity to
some foods and under emotional pressure will experience
gastric pain.

The thumb, in addition to a slight outward bend of the tip, is
of the offset type, indicating some ability for sports or a won-
derful sense of rhythm and timing. At the beginning of his
career, Warmoth was a good enough dancer to appear on the
stage in New York.

An unusual mind, and a distinctively different career.

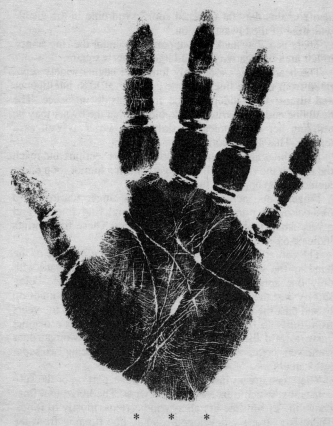

*   *   *

Michaela's hand is a female hand of the action type. Note the rounded palm, widespread fingers, and moderate number of lines.

This is an example of an extremely outwardly tilted thumb, indicating a very outgoing individual. The longer tips on the ring and little fingers would suggest the teacher, which is her profession. The index and ring finger share the dominance, an uncommon occurrence, although the index is much longer. It also contains the "fat-fingered cook" syndrome in the visible widening of the lowest section.

There is a "haystack" of support lines under the ring finger, in her area of creativity and a large teacher's square.

The head line is moderately long, and begins widely separated from the life line, a prime example of high intelligence and almost total independence from outside influence. The head line ends in a writer's fork, hinting that the owner may be utilizing her communication skills as a writer as well as a teacher. This also is correct.

Effort lines are evident on all lower finger sections and reach the tips on the ring and little fingers. Both a humor loop and a memory loop appear in the skin pattern.

Fingerprints include an arched index finger (curiosity), a peacock-feather loop on both middle and ring fingers, and a very small loop-arch on the little finger. These fingerprints indicate one or another area of specialization.

The career line begins very slightly on the ulnar side of the hand, in the subconscious area, and clearly runs upward with only one splice toward the middle finger, the splice being shortly past the age of thirty. The spliced portion continues up to and past the low-set head line, an area that covers the years from thirty to fifty in this hand. Past fifty, there is a distinct curve toward the ring finger, showing that this woman does some very creative work, after a period of balancing two separate careers.

There is a dream line on the lower ulnar portion of the subconscious, which dips low into the wrist. The horizontal lines above the dream line are allergy indications, mostly to foods. There is a strongly developed psychic line running from the life line and curving upward toward the base of the little finger, where a large healing stigmata is visible, along with the lines immediately beneath the little finger, of ability to use and handle financial matters. (See chapter 9.)

Support lines are also seen beneath the middle finger, indicating continuous self-education.

The hand is unusual in that no blocks appear on any finger section, and only one shark bite appears, on the base of the little finger, perhaps indicating frustration with a problem that cannot be solved.

A creative line springs off the career line about half an inch below the head line.

One unusual feature is that the life line bends outward about two-thirds of its length downward and splices itself into the career line. One of the indications of such a deviation on a major line is that the individual has, in a sense, given up personal concerns to concentrate solely on her career.

The owner of this print has been a teacher and instructor of adults, written several books and articles, and has shown creative artistic talent from a young age. The medical stigmata has in this case bestowed an interest in science of several types, rather than a career in medicine.

An interesting and unusually complex action hand, with a very distinctive thumb.

No book on hands could be complete without a left-dominant print.

This distinctively splotched handprint is that of a male of eighty-plus years of age. The star-shaped splotches reveal that he had several serious heart attacks, during one of which he actually died. He was revived by electrical shock paddles after four to five minutes, and the splotches reflect the electrical shock. They are also seen on hands that have undergone electroshock therapy for personality disorders.

Note the large and dominant thumb and index finger. The thumb is immense, with a massive base covering its third section. The lines of frustration occurred because the owner was temporarily prevented from working. They are accompanied by several severe shark bites, for the same reason.

An equally massive index finger indicates his total control of his life, yet the double-looped fingerprint provides a hint of some indecision concerning career direction.

Strong effort lines appear on all lower finger sections, with some rising to the tip of the little finger and only two on the middle finger. There are none on the index finger.

The individual concerned changed careers several times, as

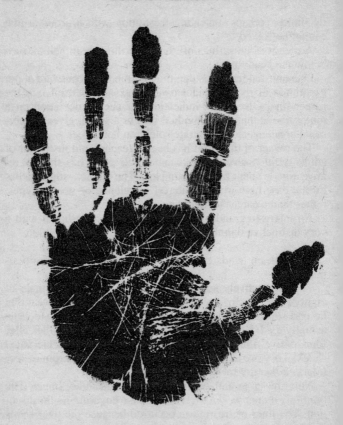

we can see from the career line, which curves upward from the ulnar side of the hand. The hand shows the electrician's skin pattern under ring and little fingers, and the owner did own an appliance repair business during the last portion of his working life. The career line provides a clue also to some more creative direction, which turned out to be a sideline business in antiques collection and sales. This is echoed by a strongly marked creative line, which runs upward into the area between ring and little fingers.

A teacher's square appears under the index finger, with a strong tip on the little finger but not an elongated one. This indicates that the individual would not be employed as a schoolteacher, but might give good advice. In the last half of his working life he devoted many hours to teaching Sunday school at his church and speaking on religion and such matters as spiritual healing and touch therapy. The shark bites on this finger are indicative of opposition he underwent as a spokesman for such a controversial subject, as well as the fact that he underwent a striking near-death experience, and was interviewed by national media on this subject. Normally a somewhat shy and retiring individual in matters of personal spirituality he used the inner power and fortitude reflected by the massive thumb and index finger to speak out publicly.

Such dominance of the radial or thumb side of the hand is most unusual, at least in this extreme form.

John's hand is unusual in that the palmar area is much more developed than the fingers.

The fingers would not be considered to be short on a hand of lesser size; they are only short compared to the length of the palm itself. The middle finger is three and a half inches long, a moderate length, but the palm is four and a half inches at the midpoint and a bit longer on the ulnar side.

This individual shows creativity in the booster lines under the ring finger, but they do not reach up to the base of the finger. They are not being used. There may be creative ideas that are not carried out. Short fingers emphasize a hasty, fast-moving person, and that may explain the problem with creativity. He is moving so fast that he never has time to act on creative ideas. There is a pressure point on the tip of this finger as well, and the finger is dominant. This indicates some problems with interpersonal relations.

There is a radial loop on the index fingertip, which echoes this tendency to hastiness. The owner is unusual in that he

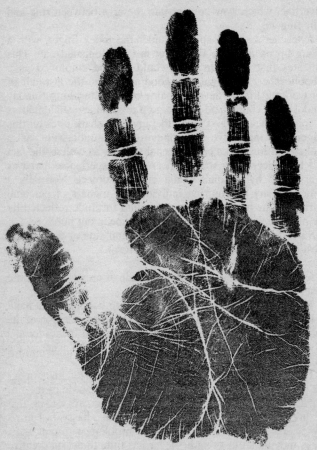

John D. age 43
Landscaper Art Collector

seeks out older persons to learn from them what they know or
have done, although he himself is young.

The thumb is as massive as is the palm, and there is con-
siderable development of the base of the palm right into the

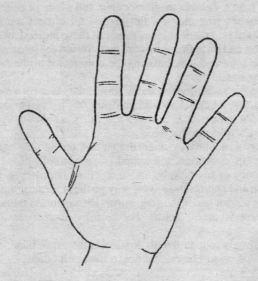

Practice Sheet

thumb. There is a visible dominance of the radial side of the palm as well, making the enormous thumb even more important.

Note that there is a double loop occupying the middle ulnar side and base of the hand. This indicates a vivid imagination, as would a whorl in that place, but it also indicates an interest in the unusual.

The career line begins under the whorl, deep in the ulnar side of the palm, and a splice appears at the head line, or age thirty. A spur line of effort strikes out from the life line and merges into the head line at approximately age thirty-nine or forty. It continues upward and eventually joins the career line under the middle finger.

An intensity line runs outward from the thumb, running clearly into the head line.

There is an L-bend in the humor area, and a loop of common sense between ring and middle fingers. An offbeat sense of humor based on practical jokes might fit these indications.

The ring and little finger tips are bent toward the middle finger of the superego, emphasizing the dominance of the radial side of the hand.

True to the radial-looped index finger, the owner is an outdoors worker, a landscaper and gardener. Yet his career direction did not appear until close to age thirty, as shown by the career line's splice at that age.

There is a secondary career, in that this young man has an extensive art collection and superb weapons collection, and spends much of his time buying and selling both items. This interest in and appreciation of art may go far to feed the unused creativity shown under the ring finger. He cannot do the work himself, for whatever reason, but he fully appreciates those who do.

The strongly looped thumb dominates the entire hand. This person must always be careful not to steamroll others.

14

SEEING THE PATTERNS

One of my associates has referred to hand analysis as a matter of seeing the pattern, somewhat like a kaleidoscope, although as in a kaleidoscope, some of the pieces are always changing.

To analyze a hand, you can pretend to be Sherlock Holmes, looking at footprints in the earth. Where has the hand been, and where is it going? You can see clearly where it has been, but to see where it is headed can only be accomplished through projection based on past and present trends.

Career directions may show up in the hand of a child as young as one year, as we have seen. Yet changes may occur during the educational process and peer group interaction that push the child in some other direction.

Parents and teachers often try to mold a child in what they feel is a good direction, yet without careful vocational aptitude analysis, they may be pushing the young person into a life of misery and longing. Despite parents' best intentions, misdirected people are found in offices everywhere you look. With modern-day downsizing and a tightened job market, it is more important than ever that you choose a career to fit your talents and continue to hone your skills through continued education and specialized classes.

SKILL INDICATORS

To provide this career direction, pay careful attention to these portions of the handprint:

Fingerprint patterns (especially index and ring fingers)
Palmar skin patterns
Finger and palm dominance
Finger section dominance
Career line direction
Booster lines beneath fingers
Teacher's square
Creative haystack
Creativity Line
Effort lines running upward on fingers

Any blocks on finger sections
Bending of fingers
Shark bites
Pressure points
Thumb dominance
Thumb bending
Length of head line
Depth of heart line
Intensity line
Heart line depth and ending area

All of these indications can only be gained from a clear, unsmudged handprint. Speedball ink is the only medium which will give you a clear print for basic analysis.

If you have any problem finding speedball ink and the rubber roller you will require, telephone an art store in your community and ask them to order these items if they do not have them.

A complete handprinting outfit will cost you ten to fifteen dollars, as you can secure a square tile to use for rolling ink for a few cents from any hardware store.

You will use ordinary typewriter paper for your handprints, although some who wish to study the subject in more depth will want to purchase a ring binder or spiral sketchpad in which to keep prints and written observations.

A tea towel or old bathroom towel will be easy to find and

will provide the necessary softening of the surface so as to print all areas of the palm, no matter how deeply it may be indented.

You may outline your prints or not, as you choose. This can be helpful at times, to clearly indicate which fingers are bending, and in which direction. I recommend that several prints be taken at one time, and that one of them may be outlined in this way.

Observations of the fingernails and the development of the back of the fingers may be made by eye, and the information transferred to the print. Remember that not only the shape of the nail, but also the color and size of the moon near its base, may be important to record.

Should you choose to print other people at work or school, family members or friends, you will find that they are often eager to give you a print and may ask many questions you cannot answer until you are experienced at hand analysis. This book and its predecessor will provide you with most of the answers you will need.

You may find many outstanding career indicators on your own hand, and a complete vocational analysis may be possible.

Good hunting.

ABOUT THE AUTHOR

Beverly "Bevy" Jaegers has studied the human hand and its various skin patterns and indications since 1961. She found most books on the hand inconclusive and at variance with one another, and so most of her work has been done in comparison analysis and intensive questioning.

Her interest in careers was sparked by a study done in 1967 with a large group of young men and women, many of whom found themselves in a profession they disliked. Others were entering college and wished to determine proper career opportunities beforehand.

Bevy's consuming interest in improving physical health through handprint analysis was sparked in 1968, when one of her public school adult education classes included a Catholic nursing sister who had access to handprints of patients in a large metropolitan hospital, as well as the diagnoses of their physicians.

Since the middle 1960s, Bevy Jaegers has written about the hand and given seminars at a number of national conferences. She is a popular guest on radio and television, and articles have appeared in many newspapers and magazines featuring her modern methods and dedication to the removal of any aspect of palmistry or fortune-telling from the subject of hand analysis.

She has founded a group of analysts and researchers and can be reached at

Hand Analysts Association
P.O. Box 29396
St. Louis, MO 63126

Her first book, *Beyond Palmistry*, (Berkley, 1992) may be found at any large bookstore.